How to Bring Your Children to Christ

...& Keep Them There

AVOIDING THE TRAGEDY OF FALSE CONVERSION

RAY COMFORT

genesis
PUBLISHING GROUP

How to Bring Your Children to Christ ... & Keep Them There

Published by
Genesis Publishing Group
2002 Skyline Place
Bartlesville, OK 74006
www.genesis-group.net

Edited by Lynn Copeland

Cover, page design, and production by Genesis Group

Printed in the United States of America

Second printing, May 2005

ISBN 0-9749300-4-0

Unless otherwise indicated, Scripture quotations are from the *New King James Version*, © 1979, 1980, 1982 by Thomas Nelson Inc., Publishers, Nashville, Tennessee.

Scripture quotations designated Amplified are from *The Amplified Bible*, © 1965 by Zondervan Publishing House, Grand Rapids, Michigan.

To my children:
Jacob, Rachel, and Daniel

their children's children

Contents

Foreword

THREE BOYS AND three girls...Chelsea and I have gone from "Growing Pains" to "The Brady Bunch." We've often wondered what will happen when our kids all enter their teens. Six teenagers—dating, driving, experimenting with life's options—all at the same time. I admit I've had the thought, *If it's true that small children have small problems and* big *kids have* big *problems, then in ten years I'm going to fake my own death and move to Tahiti!*

Growing up in this world of ungodly values and immoral lifestyles, our kids are already facing difficult challenges, and it is our responsibility as parents to give them a solid foundation upon which they can build their lives, dreams, and convictions. I find great comfort in this wonderful proverb: "Train up a child in the way he should go, and when he is old he will not depart from it" (Proverbs 22:6).

As much as I'd love for this verse of Scripture to be a guarantee of perfect Christian children as long as we raise them in a godly home, I know it doesn't always work that

7

way. Many godly parents in the Bible had sons and daughters who did not walk with the Lord. But I do know that the principle of preparing the soil for the seed of the gospel can and should start when a child is young. And I believe that the promise of this verse is that if a child learns to turn from sin and trust in Jesus when he is young, then as he grows old he will not depart from his Savior because God has already set him apart for His own glory.

Since we know that only the Holy Spirit can transform our children from the cute little "me-centered" people that they are into God-loving, God-fearing followers of Christ, the question is: What should *I* be doing as a parent? How can I "train my child" in the "way he should go" so that he will continue on God's path and become a lifelong disciple of Jesus Christ?

My good friend and ministry partner, Ray Comfort, has crafted this book utilizing a solid scriptural foundation to help you bring your children to Christ... and keep them there. Ray addresses issues beyond the initial conversion experience and provides additional ideas and practical examples of how to help keep your children from getting off course. There is no greater goal for us as parents than the eternal well-being of our children.

Ray and I have a mutual friend, Mark Waters, whom we asked to write about a very moving and powerful experience. Please read his words prayerfully:

On April 7, 2001, the unthinkable happened. It was a beautiful sunny day and my wife and I were out in the backyard taking pictures with our son, Sam (who at the time was almost four), and our daughter, Delaney (who was sixteen months old). After the hot Florida sun became unbearable, we went inside to cool off.

I had been playing with Sam in the living room and I assumed Delaney was with my wife, Becky, in the bedroom. After awhile I called out, "Is Delaney with you?" "I thought she was with you," Becky answered. My blood ran cold. It had been too long not to have heard or seen her. I knew that she had become increasingly curious about the lake behind the house so I instantly sprinted out the back door toward the lake.

As I came over the top of the hill I saw her. That vivid, horrible image will remain burned in my mind until the day I die. There was our sweet Delaney floating face down about ten feet out from shore. "Oh my God!" I yelled. Not breaking stride, I ran down the hill to the shore and with one bound I reached her. "Call an ambulance!" I yelled again. I carried her to shore and laid her pale, limp body in the grass. Our neighbor, an ex-marine, ran over and immediately began CPR on her, but I knew it was too late. I fell to the ground and from the bottom of my soul and with all the strength I had in me, I wailed.

I don't know if you've ever actually *wailed* before —I hadn't until that day. I had *cried*, I had *wept*, I would even say that I had *agonized*. But until that moment had never *wailed*. I can still hear it. How awful it sounded. I could write a hundred books and never adequately describe how I felt. I would only argue that that is the lowest point a human can reach during this lifetime. Once you reach that point, as you would imagine, you never look at anything in life the same way again.

I'm a real "bottom line" type of guy, so let me tell you what my bottom line is now that this experience is a part of my life. I have two sons now. *My life's number one goal is to lead my sons to a saving faith in Jesus Christ.* What else is there? A hundred years from now it won't matter whether they drove a tow truck or the space shuttle. They'll be dead just like Delaney. The only important question is, will they be with Delaney and Becky and me in heaven, or will they be in hell? A hundred years from now, where will your kids be? Where will *you* be?

It has been my pleasure to have Kirk Cameron's friendship for almost fifteen years. He is an incredible example of a loving husband and father, and a loyal friend. He and his family embraced us in our tragedy and for that my family and I are forever grateful.

More important, Kirk and his ministry partner, Ray Comfort, are wholly committed to fulfilling the command of Jesus Christ to "go into all the world and preach the gospel." That's not only their message, but their mission. In other words, this is what they do, not just what they tell others to do. I also know they would both tell you that this mission starts first and foremost in their own homes.

Since Delaney died—I've said this countless times but it never seems to lose its potency—as much as it hurts when I replay in my mind the events of April 7th, I can live with that. I can live the rest of my life here on earth without my precious little Delaney, and I can bear it. She's well taken care of. In fact I'll never have one single worry about her again. She's in heaven; that's a done deal and not even Satan can take that away. What I can't bear is the thought of spending eternity without any one of my children. I love them too much not to devote my life to leading them toward a saving faith in Jesus Christ.

I don't think that I love my kids any more or less than anyone else. I'm no super dad, or super Christian for that matter. But God has given me a perspective in my life that not everyone shares, and for that I'm thankful, and I intend to do something about it. Life is too short not to.

In picking up this book, you obviously are concerned about the spiritual life of your children. Nothing is more important than where they will spend eternity. Although as parents we each have our own style of communicating and relating with our children, there are foundational biblical guidelines that we all must follow if we hope to have God's blessings upon our parental toil and tears. Ray has masterfully drawn out these basic guidelines from God's training manual for children—The Bible. I encourage you to read, pray about, and put into practice these very helpful tips so that you can guide your children to genuinely embrace Jesus and stay with Him forever.

Blessings on your journey,

Kirk Cameron

Introduction

Y OU MAY HAVE wondered about the scriptural soundness of the title *How to Bring Your Children to Christ...and Keep Them There*. Of course, any theologian will tell you that we can't "bring" our children to Christ, and neither can we "keep them there." Both are strictly the work of God's grace. However, my alternative title was *How to Biblically Plant the Seed of the Everlasting Gospel in the Hearts of Your Children, Having Complete Assurance That God is Faithful and Will Save All Who Call Upon His Name...Knowing Also That in His Great Goodness He Will Keep Them from Falling, Presenting Them Faultless Before the Presence of His Glory with Exceeding Joy.* That was rather unwieldy, so I took the liberty of using a shorter title.

While there is no sure-fire formula to secure the salvation of any human being, the Bible assures us that if a child truly repents and trusts the Savior, God will begin a good work in him that He will complete. Our role as parents is to ensure that he is truly born of God, rather than of the will of man. Too many within the Church think all that is necessary for any child to be saved is for him to "ask Jesus into his heart." That may sound like good doctrine, but it's not biblical. This misunderstanding of the necessity of genuine conversion usually comes from an unawareness of the reality of false conversion.

After I had spoken at a church recently, a woman excitedly told me that her eight-year-old had been eyeing the communion juice. She informed him, "You can't take communion until you have Jesus in your heart"—he then "asked Jesus into his heart" so he could have the juice.

While many of today's converts come to Jesus for the "juice" of promised benefits, the biblical motive for coming to the Savior is that we have sinned against God, and therefore need mercy. Someone once said, "The most important thing that parents can teach their children is how to get along without them." That's true...in this life. We do want our children to be able to stand on their own two feet. However, there is something infinitely more important: where they will spend eternity—in heaven or in hell. A misunderstanding of biblical conversion can do great damage to that cause.

Anyone, including a child, who comes to Jesus must have knowledge of sin and exercise biblical repentance. When a child fails to find that place of true repentance, we shouldn't therefore be surprised when he "falls away" from the faith as he encounters the temptations of the world. My prayer is that this publication will help you guide your children toward true conversion.

The intent of this book, however, isn't simply to help you teach your children about the things of God. It is my hope that God will use this book to raise up laborers—a generation who will carry out the Great Commission.

For that reason, we also recommend a companion publication called *The Way of the Master for Kids*. This book teaches children how to memorize the Ten Commandments in only five minutes, so they will remember them for life. It also shows them how to refute the theory of evolution, prove the existence of God, and answer questions such as "Who made God?" and "Why is there suffering?" Your children will not only understand salvation, but be able to share and defend their faith.

May God bless you and give you wisdom as you instruct your children in the most important of life's issues.

Perhaps a Six-Foot Drop

SOMETHING WONDERFUL happens when a giraffe is born. It drops about six feet to the ground, stands up, wobbles for around an hour, and then begins walking behind its mother. No diapers. No potty training. No learning to crawl and then walk. It has arrived, and in one hour it's ready to go.

Why couldn't it be that way for people? Human offspring are virtually helpless until they are eighteen years old. Perhaps if there were a six-foot drop at birth...

The fact that our children are helpless, however, does not mean that we as parents are. In His Word, God has given us plenty of assistance to guide us as we steer our children through their often tumultuous teens to become godly young men and women.

My wife, Sue, and I raised three children. When they were young, sincere folk warned us that we should expect our kids to become rebellious during their teenage years. It didn't happen. They never brought us a moment of grief, and we believe this was simply because we adhered to certain guidelines and principles from God's Word.

Of course, these principles are not an absolute guarantee that children won't become rebellious and turn their backs on the things of God. But they worked for us, and it is our earnest prayer that they work for you and those who are most precious to you.

Perfect Timing

On a flight from Los Angeles to Atlanta, Georgia, I spoke to the man seated next to me and shared a little about the television show that I co-host with Kirk Cameron. He mentioned that he had studied psychology, so I said, "Hey, Steve. I've got a question for you in light of your interest in psychology. Kirk and I often ask this question of people on our TV show. What do you think is on the other side... what do you think happens after you die?"

He thought for a moment, then answered, "Nothing." I asked, "Are you an atheist?" He replied that he was, so I said, "Could you believe me if I told you that this plane came together by accident? Its jet engines, windows, seats, and wings were not built; they came from nothing and fell together." He actually said he could believe that! With that answer, I decided it was best to quickly move from his professed intellect to his conscience, and went through the Ten Commandments with him. (Holding up God's holy standard will show a self-righteous person that he isn't as good as he thinks he is—a principle we'll look at in-depth later in the book.)

After realizing that he had broken four of the Ten Commandments, he admitted that if God were to judge him by that standard, he would end up in hell. When I asked, "Does that concern you?" he quickly answered that it didn't concern him at all.

I then told him about a friend of mine who at the age of twenty learned he had terminal cancer. His other friends advised him to enjoy his last six months by spending it with prostitutes. He wasn't interested, because he had something stronger than his sex drive—it was his will to live. A cry came from within his heart, *Oh, I don't want to die!*

By this time the passenger seated next to Steve had tuned in, so I pointed to him and said, "God has given you that same will to live." I looked at the professing atheist and earnestly said, "He has also given you the will to live, Steve." Just then the plane, which had begun a slow descent, suddenly revved its engines, and in a split second changed to a steep ascent. This had the terrifying effect of throwing the passengers into a momentary, nauseating weightlessness. Faces were filled with alarm and several passengers shouted out in fear. I looked at Steve and commented, "That sure kicked in the will to live." Stunned, he replied, "Absolutely!"

The timing was perfect. From that point on, he listened to everything I had to say, and even accepted one of my books. There are no atheists in an air pocket.

I don't know if God caused the plane to do that at that precise moment, but there comes a time in the life of a Christian when "coincidences" occur so often, it becomes illogical to use the word. The timing was perfect, and that's the way God works. His timing is always perfect. He's never late for anything. What may seem to be too late, isn't. Red Seas can be opened, lions' mouths can be shut, and even the dead can be resurrected. Nothing is ever hopeless, because with God nothing is impossible. So never panic about the spiritual life of your children. Ask God for their salvation, then thank Him for it. Rest in the Lord. Trust Him. Faith never loses its peace; it sleeps even in a storm.

> No one can come to the Son unless the Father draws him. So you don't want to run ahead of the Lord and lead your children into a false conversion.

There is a right timing for the conversion of each of your children. That timing is in God's hands. They won't come to Christ before that time, because they can't. No one can come to the Son unless the Father draws him (John 6:44). So you don't want to run ahead of the Lord and lead your children into a false conversion (a crucial principle that we will explore in Chapter 6).

I learned about God's timing the hard way. Back in my native country of New Zealand in 1982, I discovered the use of the Law (the Ten Commandments) as the God-given tool to reach the lost.[1] I had complete faith that He would open doors for me to teach this principle in the United States.[2] In 1987, through a series of circumstances, Sue and I found ourselves in Southern California, so I arranged to hold a seminar. Convinced that I was in the right place, I did a little publicity and sat back to watch God bring things together.

The day of the seminar, I arrived at the venue, expecting a crowd. See if you can guess how many people showed up. Zip. *No one.* Not a soul. I was at the right place, at the wrong time. I said to the man who drove me to the location, "This is God's way of telling me that I'm running ahead of Him. I need to wait for His timing. Let's get out of here." We quickly closed the door and left.

Less than two years later, doors that I didn't open suddenly opened for us. Without any effort on our part, we were invited to live in the U.S. where we were given a rent-free home, a car, and a generous salary (as pastor of evangelism), and all of our insurance was paid for us. That taught me that God has a right timing for certain things, and it is a big mistake to run ahead of Him, even if we are sincere.

God is not willing that your children perish. He wants them to come to repentance. Here's how you can know that:

> The Lord is not slack concerning His promise, as some count slackness, but is longsuffering toward us, not willing that any should perish but that all should come to repentance. (2 Peter 3:9)

There are some who try to qualify this verse to fit a certain interpretation of Scripture, but at face value the words "any" and "all" include your children. Scripture also says that God wants *all* to be saved and to come to the knowledge of the truth (1 Timothy 2:4). Add to that the fact that Jesus said, "All things, whatever you ask in prayer, believing, you will receive" (Matthew 21:22), and there you have it. It is simple. Do you believe that when God's Word says He wants *all* to be saved that He means *all*, and that *anything* you ask in prayer believing, you shall receive? These are promises from a God who *cannot* lie. So if there is any promise on which you and I should stand firm, it's for God to work toward the salvation of our children.

I don't believe in the "name it and claim it" prosperity message, which is motivated by covetousness. However, it is based on some truth. Jesus said, "Have faith in God." If you doubt His Word, the Bible says that you are calling God a liar (see 1 John 5:10). Doubt produces fear, worry, and concern. It steals peace and joy. Faith, on the other hand, will actually *produce* peace and joy. The choice of whether to trust God is ours. When we ask for what is in accordance with His will, we can confidently trust God to be at work in the lives of our children, drawing them toward the Savior.

Think of it as you would a healthy pregnancy. The seed is first planted in the womb. Then God causes the miracle of gestation. During the growth period, all that is needed is for the mother to provide the proper nutrients for her developing child, and to keep away from poisons such as drugs, alcohol, and cigarettes. When the baby is ready, the birth will happen at the right time.

The Tragic Error

Jesus said that one must be born again in order to see the kingdom of God (John 3:3). So let's now talk about this spiritual pregnancy. For your children to be born again, you want to be sure to plant the good seed of the pure Word of God (1 Peter 1:23). You also need to ensure that you stay away from toxins that will cause a stillbirth.

It's essential that you become familiar with the biblical reality of true and false conversion. Do not assume that everyone who names the name of Christ is genuinely saved. Many Christians make this tragic error.

Children are particularly vulnerable when it comes to false conversions. This is usually because parents and children's workers are not aware that there is such a thing as spurious (false) conversion. They have "zeal without knowledge." We may be zealous in our desire to fly a plane, but it is dangerous to do so without the right knowledge.

Having zeal when it comes to bringing our children to Christ is understandable. Each of us should rightly be concerned for their welfare—particularly their *eternal* welfare —so it makes sense that we want them to be converted at an early age. However, I have received numerous letters from grieved parents who say that their children were "converted" at a very young age, but have since strayed into drugs, alcohol, sex, etc., usually in their teenage years.

It is likely that these children had false conversions, a fact that was made evident when temptation came their way. A plant may seem healthy, but a burning hot sun will cause it to whither and die if it has a faulty root system or is in shallow soil.

Sue and I weren't seeking a "decision for Christ" from our children. Decisions are easy to get. All you have to do is gather a group of children and ask, "Kids, how do you live forever?" "By giving your heart to Jesus!" "Who wants to give their heart to Jesus?" A sea of hands wave—fifty decisions. The problem is that they will be fine until teenage temptation reveals their unconverted condition. All this "decision" accomplishes is giving the children, and ourselves, a false sense of assurance.

In addressing parents, Dr. Robert A. Morey says,

> Another possible snare you must avoid at all costs is the blind faith of some parents. Now, it is clear that Christian parents should desire that their children come to know and love the Lord Jesus early in life. This desire is one evidence that *they* are saved. A parent who claims to be saved but does not manifest any concern to see his children saved is no more saved than a stone.
>
> While the desire to see your children saved is proper and necessary, some parents become so desperate

to believe that their children are saved that they will grasp at anything. Even when their son or daughter openly denies the faith and engages in gross wickedness, they will still comfort themselves by saying, "Well, at least my son is saved. He may not act like it now but I know he is saved because he accepted Jesus when he was five years old. He doesn't go to church anymore and married [someone from another religion] but I still say he is saved."

Instead of facing the reality that their child is on his way to hell, some parents will cling to false hopes so they can sleep at night. But instead of seeking their own psychological comfort, they should seek the conversion of their child by telling him the truth.[3]

> "Instead of facing the reality that their child is on his way to hell, some parents will cling to false hopes so they can sleep at night."

The truth is that, for any child (or adult) to be saved, there must be an understanding of the nature of sin. He must turn from his sin and trust in Jesus to save him. Eternal life comes not from saying a prayer or making a decision, but from "repentance toward God and faith toward our Lord Jesus Christ" (Acts 20:21).

Genuine salvation must be a work of God. We can have as much a part in the spiritual birth of our children as we have in the planting of a tree. We can prepare the soil and water the seed, but it will grow only if God sees fit to cause it to do so. All we can do is make ready the soil of the child's heart, plant the pure seed of the Word of God, keep away harmful influences, and faithfully water it with believing prayer.

We'll look at the first step of preparation in our next chapter.

After Your Own Kind

T HE FOLLOWING information may be of interest to you: A new scientific study has revealed that, if your parents didn't have children, neither will you. This points out a biblical reality, a pattern that God has established: we produce after our own kind.

If we want to raise godly children, the best way to achieve this is to be godly parents. Whether we like it or not, our children will tend to follow our examples—both good and bad. What kind of example are you setting? Are you careful to watch your own behavior so you're a godly role-model for your children?

If you truly want your children to come to Christ and stay there, begin by making sure that you fulfill the requirements of Psalm 1. The key to having your children respect what you say is for them to respect the one who is doing the saying. Nothing dissipates respect like hypocrisy. I would rather lose my right arm than have one of my children consider me a hypocrite. So let's search out God's Word, and at the same time, let the Word search us.

Blessed Is the Man...

In Psalm 1, Scripture gives us a clear picture of what a godly person should be, as well as the reward of this godliness.

> Blessed is the man who walks not in the counsel of the ungodly, nor stands in the path of sinners, nor sits in the seat of the scornful; but his delight is in the law of the Lord, and in His law he meditates day and night. He shall be like a tree planted by the rivers of water, that brings forth its fruit in its season, whose leaf also shall not wither; and whatever he does shall prosper. (vv. 1–3)

Let's meditate on these verses to truly understand their meaning and consider how they apply to parenting.

God says that you are blessed (highly favored) if you don't listen to the world's advice. If you are tempted to heed the "counsel of the ungodly," consider that the world's "experts" believe mankind evolved from monkeys. A little thought on our part should help us see why it's wise not to listen to their ramblings, but rather listen to what the Creator has to say.

The fruit of the world's godless advice is seen in the headlines of the daily news. Their counsel may sound right, but so often it proves to be wrong. For example, the world says that if you love your children, you will never physically

28

discipline them. It says to seek alternatives rather than inflicting physical pain.

In the Book of Proverbs, written by the wisest man who ever lived, God's Word gives the following counsel:

> Foolishness is bound up in the heart of a child, but the rod of correction will drive it far from him. (Proverbs 22:15)

> The rod and reproof give wisdom, but a child left to himself brings shame to his mother. (Proverbs 29:15)

It's commonly said that he who spares the rod spoils the child, but God's Word actually puts it more strongly:

> He who spares his rod *hates* his son, but he who loves him disciplines him promptly. (Proverbs 13:24, emphasis added)

So there's your choice: listen to what *seems* right, or do what God says *is* right.

As parents, we should always do what the Word of God says to do, and often that's not easy. Applying the rod of correction (often called "the board of education") to "the seat of learning" takes resolution, as well as courage. But love will do it. The Bible says that in doing so you will save your children from hell (see Proverbs 23:13,14), and what parents want their children to go to hell? We should value the eternal welfare of our children, rather than our own temporal anxiety when it comes to applying discipline.

The contrast between God's ways and the world's ways was clearly demonstrated in an incident that occurred when our eldest son, Jacob, was six years old. We had a neighbor who would never even *think* of physically disciplining her six-year-old. When he refused to go to school, she would simply bribe him with candy.

One day Jacob said a word to his mother that he wasn't supposed to say. I sent him to his room, and then followed him a moment later. I asked him if he knew that what he said was wrong. He admitted that he did. I then told him to bend over his bed, and resolutely gave him a swift swat across his rear with a small stick. He burst into tears. I went to get him a tissue, then left him alone for ten minutes. When I returned, I knelt down in front of him and hugged him. I then looked him in the eyes and said, "I want you to pray and ask God to forgive you, then go out to your mother and tell her that you are sorry." He did just that.

A few minutes later I was helping Sue dry the dishes while Jacob sat at the table, thoughtfully holding a pencil and paper. Suddenly I felt a tug on my shirt. It was Jacob. He reached up and handed me a note. It read: "I love my dad."

This made no sense to me. I had just caused him physical pain, yet even as a six-year-old he could discern that my motive was love.

In contrast, the neighbor's six-year-old would point a toy gun at his mother and say, "I hate you, I hate you. I'm going to kill you!" Of course, he wasn't disciplined for that either.

Tragically, the world refuses to use the rod of correction to drive "foolishness" from the hearts of their children. The foolishness therefore remains in their hearts as they grow, and many children bring their parents nothing but grief by ending up pregnant, in prison, with drug or alcohol problems, or with broken marriages.

The Composer

I was once discussing music with Carol and Stuart Scott, who are part of our television production team, when Carol casually mentioned, "Scotty has written a few songs." I then asked Scotty to sing one of his compositions. He was a little reluctant at first, but with some goading he began to sing a song he had written. It was from Psalm 27:4: "One thing have I desired of the LORD, that I will seek after; that I may dwell in the house of the LORD all the days of my life, to behold the beauty of the LORD, and to inquire in His temple." Tears immediately welled up in my eyes. The song he had composed was a worldwide megahit, and one with which I was intimately familiar. We had learned it many years earlier, way down under in New Zealand—7,000 miles away.

I'm sure if Carol hadn't told me that Scotty had written it, I would have gently corrected him as he sung its words.

His beginning was slightly different from the famous Mara-natha arrangement.[4] However, once I knew he was the song's composer, I dared not say a word. After all, it was *his* song.

The ungodly think that they can ignore the Bible and call the tune on all of life's issues. They are self-appointed experts. They don't realize that God is the author of all things, and that we dare not even whisper a word of correction. Besides, humanity's godless arrangement hasn't given us harmony, but chaos in almost every area. They see prayer as a *last* resort, when it should be our first. They say that God *isn't* to be feared, when to fear Him is the beginning of wisdom. They think God is their friend, when He's their enemy. They think they are morally good, when God says they are morally corrupt. They think they are heading for heaven, when the Word of God says that they are heading for hell. They are the willfully deaf and blind trying to lead the deaf and blind. Don't follow them.

God is the composer of life itself, so listen to His words and His words alone, and then be blessed by refusing to walk in "the counsel of the ungodly," particularly when it comes to raising your precious kids.

Friend or Foe?

Let's continue our look at Psalm 1. Verse 1 also informs us: *We are blessed if we don't stand in the path of sinners.* Be separate from this sinful world. Jesus was, yet He was still accused of being a "friend of sinners." In other words, don't withdraw from the world and become "holier than thou." It is easy to look at this proud, self-righteous generation and become cynical and condescending, but we must remember that we too were once deceived. So come apart from their sins, but mingle with the lost for the sake of their salvation. As Christians, we are to be "without fault in the midst of a crooked and perverse generation, among whom you shine as lights in the world" (Philippians 2:15). Notice our involvement with the lost: "in the midst...among...in the world." Remember that the reason we are in the world is to "shine as lights."

We must not "stand in the path of sinners" because the Bible warns that without holiness, no one will see the Lord (see Hebrews 12:14). To live in holiness means to be separate from the sin that is in the world. How do you know if you are living in holiness? To judge whether you are a "friend" of the world, and therefore an enemy of God, ask yourself if you love the things He loves and hate the things He hates.

Keep in mind that what you may consider a casual acquaintance with the sinful world may be seen as blatant hypocrisy by your children. If your desires are for entertainment that glorifies sex and violence, then you should question whether you are standing with the world or with the Lord. Every time you compromise your Christian walk in front of your children, you are causing the word "hypocrite" to enter their tender minds.

Name Your Price

A good friend once called me and said that he had been offered a movie deal, but had a problem with part of the script. The story line was wonderful, but as usual in a romantic movie, it included a passionate kiss. He would get $100,000 for his role in the movie, but he said, "I won't kiss another woman like that, and besides, what would my kids think of me if they saw the movie?" He turned down the part, not only because using a stand-in would still have had an "appearance of evil," but because it could have undermined his testimony for the gospel.

I greatly respect him for taking this stand. Think of it. Could you bring yourself to kiss someone other than your spouse for ten seconds—for $100,000?

The incident reminded me of a story I heard of an English prime minister who, during a dinner, leaned over to the woman seated next to him and asked, "Would you go to bed with me for a million dollars?" She answered, "I would think about it." He then asked, "Would you go to bed with me for one dollar?" She widened her eyes and said indignantly, "What kind of woman do you think I am!" He replied, "Madam, we have already established that. Now we are just negotiating the price."

For what amount of money would you "prostitute" yourself? What price tempts you to compromise your Christian walk? $100,000? $1? God isn't impressed with the amount, and neither should we be impressed or even tempted. Each of us should have the mindset that we wouldn't compromise our integrity and cause our children to stumble for any amount of money.

The Christian life is one of self-denial. We are to deny ourselves the pleasures of sin. It is all too easy to sit back and feed on movies that are filled with sinful excitement, but the key to resisting temptation is the sight of Calvary's cross. Did you see the movie *The Passion of the Christ*? As I watched the crucifixion scene, my palms began to sweat and I started to hyperventilate, it was so brutal. In most movies, violent scenes are over in a moment, but in *The Passion of the Christ*, it went on, and on, and on. While there was some artistic license taken in the movie, the brutality was based on what actually happened to Jesus of Nazareth. The Bible says that He was "marred more than any man" and was "bruised for our iniquities."

The cross should be ever before us, and the result will be an identification with it: "those who are Christ's have crucified the flesh with its passions and desires" (Galatians 5:24). It cost the blood of God's only Son to purchase our redemption. How then could we willfully sin against God after such a display of love? To do so would be to despise His sacrifice. We therefore must determine to put to death our sinful desires and no longer "stand in the path of sinners."

We are blessed if we don't sit in the seat of the scornful. Christians don't have time to "sit." We once "sat in the shadow of death," but no longer. Now we have an urgent task before us: to seek those who are still in that shadow. When Jesus said, "My food is to do the will of Him who sent Me" (John 4:34), He was referring to seeking the lost. Is that our primary motivation on earth—to do the will of God? If not, then how can we call ourselves followers of Christ? We are told to "imitate" Him, and He was consumed with reaching the unsaved. Are we?

> If we are worldly and undisciplined, our kids may grow up to follow our poor example. If we are hypocrites, we may just reproduce hypocrites.

We probably live in the most self-indulgent generation that ever professed spirituality. The messages of contemporary Christianity are often about self. Many pastors preach on how we can obtain what is rightfully ours in Christ, but fail to speak about the dreadful fate of the lost. Rarely do they call for Christians to pray for the salvation of those around them, let alone *speak* to them about the issue. The eternal salvation of the world should devour our thoughts, and if it doesn't, something is radically wrong.

We are also not to "scorn" the things of God. The Bible teaches that the lost hate God "without cause." They use as a cuss word the holy name of the God who gave them life, and they mock godliness. To them, the uncompromising Christian is puritanical and narrow-minded. And so we should be. Only the pure in heart will see God, and according to Jesus, the way to life is narrow. We are not to walk, stand, or sit with this world, because we are not of this world.

We are blessed if we delight in the law of the Lord and meditate on it daily. Is your delight in God's Word? Do you read the Bible *daily*? That means *every* day without fail. Each of us should say to ourselves, "No Bible, no breakfast. No read, no feed." Be like Job, who "treasured the words of His mouth *more* than [his] necessary food" (Job 23:12, emphasis added). The key is to put your Bible before your belly—to seek *first* the kingdom of God and His righteousness.

If we are not "disciples" of Christ—disciplined to His Word—we will more than likely reproduce after our own kind. If we are worldly and undisciplined, our kids may grow up to follow our poor example of what a Christian should be. If we are hypocrites, we may just reproduce hypocrites. What greater parental betrayal could there be than to lead your children to hell? So esteem God's Word more than your necessary food, and teach your kids to do the same.

Lack of Knowledge

A friend of mine named Luis spent two and a half weeks in England evangelizing for a new church that had been planted there by his home church in California. On his way back to the States, he decided to spend the night in London so he could visit London's famous museum. As he strolled by an underground rail system, a young homeless woman walked alongside him and asked him for some change.

Suddenly she reached into Luis's shoulder bag. He quickly grabbed her wrist, told her to let go of whatever she was holding in the bag, and yelled to passersby to call the police. But to his surprise no one took any notice.

The woman wouldn't let go. Neither would Luis. He didn't know if she had hold of his passport, his car keys, or his money. It was a dark area, so he decided he needed to move into better lighting. He grabbed the woman's jacket sleeve and began dragging her with him toward the light.

As he noticed other homeless folk moving toward him, the situation began to get scary. The woman then slipped out of her jacket, left it in his hands, and ran off with what she was holding onto: about eighty English pounds.

Luis soon found a police officer, who informed him that he was in a bad part of town and should go home. But Luis didn't have a home. He was now "homeless," because he had just been robbed of the money he was planning to use to get a hotel for the night.

He walked the dark streets for the next six hours, in a storm with high winds. His feet were sore. He was miserable. He was cold, hungry, and sleep deprived.

In a pouch he was wearing around his waist, however, he had three hundred U.S. dollars. He didn't try to use the money for food or a hotel room because he didn't realize that American currency was good all over the world.

As Christian parents we can be like Luis. He was cold, hungry, and tired simply because he lacked knowledge. Had he known the power of the American dollar, he could have had warm food and a comfortable bed. But he didn't.

Do you realize the wealth of knowledge God has given you in His Word? Do you draw on that wealth? Do you say with David, "I rejoice at Your word as one who finds great treasure" (Psalm 119:162)? The Bible contains knowledge that will save you and your children a great deal of pain. If you don't know where the dark areas of this life are, you will walk right into them. So let God's Word give you light. Read, memorize, and teach your family from the Book of Proverbs. It was written to provide wisdom, instruction, knowledge, discretion, and understanding.

And always remember that the thief came to steal, kill, and destroy. If you let him get his grubby hands into your family's life through music, entertainment, ungodly counsel, or by any other means, he won't let go. So listen to God's wisdom—stay out of that part of town and teach your children to do likewise.

The Prosperity Message

When you daily draw on the wealth of knowledge in God's Word, there is one biblical promise of "prosperity" that you can truly claim:

> He shall be like a tree planted by the rivers of water, that brings forth its fruit in its season, whose leaf also shall not wither; and whatever he does shall prosper. (Psalm 1:3)

39

If you do as Psalm 1 instructs, the Scriptures promise that you will be like a tree that is planted by rivers of water. Notice that the tree is "planted." It is not a wild tree randomly sprouting up, but is the planting *of the Lord*—a tree of righteousness (see Isaiah 61:3). Notice also that the tree is planted by *rivers* of water. Rather than relying on a single river that could dry up, it's planted by multiple rivers for an abundant source of life-giving moisture. In Christ, you will never lack living water.

A tree that is planted by rivers of water is deep-rooted. You won't be torn up by the roots when the winds of tribulation blow. Trials will just encourage your roots to grow deeper into God and will make you stronger.

You will also bring forth fruit in season (love, joy, peace, patience, etc.); your leaf will not wither (you will retain effervescence and vitality as a Christian); and *whatever you do will prosper*. That "whatever" includes your marriage, your vocation, your evangelistic endeavors...and the raising of your family.

In our next chapter, we'll look at how spending family times together can help your children develop spiritual roots that will enable them to bring forth lasting fruit.

Chapter Three

What's on Their Mind?

Y EARS AGO, AFTER open-air preaching to a crowd, I was speaking to some non-Christians about the things of God. My eight-year-old daughter, Rachel, was standing quietly beside me as I spoke.

Suddenly she whispered, "Dad!" I ignored her because I was speaking about eternal things; what she had to say could wait. Besides, I had taught her not to interrupt an adult conversation unless it was an emergency.

Twice more I heard a quiet, "Dad...Dad!" I continued speaking, but I reached out my firm fatherly fingers and gently patted my daughter on her warm little head. This was to let her know that I had heard her, and that I'd only be a moment. It was then that I realized what was on her mind. She had been hit squarely on the head by an incoming sea gull.

The test of your relationship with your children comes when one of life's "sea gulls" strikes them. Who do they go to for help? If you want it to be you, it's very important that you take the time now to cultivate a loving relationship.

In November 2004, CBS News cited a recent study showing that children who ate regular meals with their parents were less likely to smoke cigarettes, drink alcohol, take drugs, get depressed, or commit suicide. Even the world can see the benefit of spending meal times together as a family. During these informal gatherings, you not only communicate with those you love, but you share personal time with them. Talk with your kids about the world in general and their world in particular, how their parents met, how they were as babies, school, and a million other topics. Get to know your children, and help them learn more about their parents, each other, and their family history. Otherwise, your family members are in danger of becoming passing strangers within your home.

Make the effort to open the hearts of your children, deliberately drawing them out of themselves. Let the conversation swing to what they have done that day, allowing them to express their desires and thoughts. Show interest in *their* interests. If you want to build your relationship and make lifelong friends of your children, start while they are young. Don't wait until they are teenagers to do this. It may be too late.

If you demonstrate interest in their small, everyday concerns, they will come to you and let you know what's on their mind when their concerns become bigger.

Take the Lead

Among the many topics you talk about with your children, the most important one is God. Too many parents consider the church to have the primary responsibility for spiritually training their kids. But the responsibility lies on your shoulders. If you are a father, take the lead in teaching your children about the things of the Lord; don't leave it up to your wife. Consider the command of Scripture:

> And, you, fathers, do not provoke your children to wrath, but bring them up in the training and admonition of the Lord. (Ephesians 6:4)

Perhaps you feel inadequate to lead. If so, be aware that pride will often masquerade as a feeling of inadequacy. Humble yourself. Forget what your wife thinks. Forget what your kids think. Forget what you think about your inabilities. Your only concern should be what God thinks. If you are a single parent, step into the role of the leader.

It's interesting to note that when the Bible tells fathers to bring their children up "in the training and admonition of the Lord," it doesn't give detailed instructions. There's not much explicit, practical teaching in Scripture on how to do this. It just says to do it.

Think about your instincts as a parent. Did anyone have to tell you how to raise your children? There were certain things that you knew instinctively to do. You must feed, clothe, house, and educate your kids. You don't want to leave them cold, hungry, destitute, and illiterate. You taught them that fire burns, water drowns, and if they climb they may fall. What you learned by experience and what you possessed by instinct, you intuitively passed on to those you love.

The same applies spiritually. If you love your children, feed them spiritually. Clothe them in righteousness. Teach them the importance of clothing themselves in humility. Educate them about what will harm them in this life and in the next. What you have learned by experience about spiritual things, deliberately pass on to your children. If you are shallow spiritually, then your instruction to your children will be shallow, so deepen your own walk with the Lord. Be sensitive to what pleases God. Have your senses *exercised* to discern both good and evil (see Hebrews 5:14). Whatever your conscience instinctively tells you about moral issues, pass on to those you love.

One of the best ways to do this and build godly principles into the lives of your children is through an intentional time dedicated to that goal—a daily family devotional time.

Heavy Rocks of Resolution

In Old Testament times, people sometimes built an altar to God to commemorate something He had done. Altars also served as a memorial to teach succeeding generations about God and His character.

Gathering for a family "altar" or a devotional time is a good way to teach your children about God and His ways. It is essential for their spiritual growth that you *make* the time to establish a family altar. Build it out of the unmovable rocks of resolution.

The reason you will have to be resolute is that it will be a battle. You will find that there are many excuses for not having devotions. "Circumstances" will constantly crop up. You may be pressed for time, feel tired, or simply want to catch up on the news of the world. Your kids will occasionally groan when you announce that it's time for devotions. Perhaps you think you don't have the ability to teach the Bible. Loved ones may subtly, subconsciously discourage you. However, your time of family devotions should be a priority for your whole family. Don't be legalistic about it, but as much as possible, put all other things aside before you postpone or cancel your family altar.

It will literally be an altar of sacrifice, as you sacrifice your time, your energy, and sometimes your dignity. For years, our kids heard, "Six o'clock—reading time." That meant Sue and I dropped whatever we were doing, and the children learned to do the same, and we gathered together as a family. Making it a priority for your family's growth will speak volumes about its importance in their lives.

As your children get older, they will more than likely enter the "ice age," in which they will sit like blocks of ice.

Around that time you will ask yourself, "Is it worth it?" Carry on regardless. You are imparting God's Word, and He will watch over it.

Several years ago, a man wrote a letter to the editor of *The British Weekly*, questioning whether church was worthwhile. He complained that he's attended church for thirty years and heard 3,000 sermons, yet couldn't remember a single one.

His letter prompted the following response: "I have been married for thirty years. During that time I have eaten 32,850 meals—mostly of my wife's cooking. Suddenly, I have discovered that I cannot remember the menu of a single meal. And yet, I received nourishment from every single one of them. I have the distinct impression that without them, I would have starved to death long ago."

As you face distractions of various kinds, always keep in mind one very powerful reason why you should have daily devotions: the eternal salvation of your children.

With that thought in mind, here are some practical points to consider when establishing your family altar.

Open in Prayer

Begin devotions by thanking God for your family and then prayerfully asking Him, "Open my eyes, that I may see wondrous things from Your Law" (Psalm 119:18). The Bible uses the phrase "the Law" to refer at different times to the entire Word of God, the Law of Moses, and the Ten Commandments. The Ten Commandments are the very backbone of Holy Scripture. We must seek the help of God's Holy Spirit if we are to comprehend the incredible things God has in His Law. The apostle Paul said, "I delight in the Law of God" (Romans 7:22). Why should we delight in God's Law, even though we are not saved by our obedience to it? It is because the Law reveals God's holiness, His righteousness, His justice and truth. It is the very instrument that the Holy Spirit uses to convert the soul (Psalm 19:7). It is the means by which the way to the sinner's heart is prepared to receive the grace of God. If we want our children to be truly converted, we must first know the wondrous things from His Law, and that comes only by prayer and revelation of the Holy Spirit.

If you are not used to praying out loud, have everyone close their eyes while you pray so they won't see you. (Some find that less intimidating.) As time goes by, ask your children to open in prayer. They could start with a simple, "Dear Lord, please help us learn. Amen." This will help build their confidence when it comes to "public" prayer. It is wise to keep public prayer relatively brief. A short, stumbling, sincere prayer of a child is infinitely better in God's sight than long-winded, empty Pharisaical eloquence.

Read the Bible Out Loud
The Bible says, "A servant of the Lord must...be able to teach" (2 Timothy 2:24). So if you're worried about a lack

of teaching ability, don't say, "I can't teach"; say, "Success comes in *cans*." Memorize this promise from Scripture: "I can do all things through Christ who strengthens me" (Philippians 4:13). Simply start by reading five verses from one of the Gospels. Then have each of the family members read five verses; this will not only help them become more confident in reading out loud but will help them remain attentive. Pause now and then to ask what they think a particular verse means. Take a few minutes to go through the verses beforehand and prepare some questions. Be ready for (and don't be discouraged by) a regular "I dunno." Tell your children what you think the verse means, and continue with the reading, making use of any Bible cross-references.

> "Let us never be guilty, as parents, of forgetting the religious training of our children; for if we do we may be guilty of the blood of their souls."

If you have young children, start with a "picture" Bible. I did this many years ago when I found a Bible full of beautiful pictures of Adam and Eve, Noah's ark, David and Goliath, etc. But when I turned to the New Testament, I found a picture of King Herod being presented with John the Baptist's head on a plate! John's eyes were vacantly staring into space, and his mouth was gaping open! It was horrible. So, I took some crayons, and

(God forgive me) I changed John the Baptist's head into a birthday cake. For years my kids must have been mystified about why King Herod's guests were so horrified at the sight of a cake.

An excellent book if you have kids ages three to twelve is *Little Visits with God* by Mary Manz Simon (Concordia Publishing House). Also, you may like to use *The Way of the Master for Kids* (Genesis Publishing Group).

Begin having devotions with your kids as soon as they are old enough to understand. Charles Spurgeon advises,

> Let us expect our children to know the Lord. Let us from the beginning mingle the name of Jesus with their ABC[s]. Let them read their first lessons from the Bible. It is a remarkable thing that there is no book from which children learn to read so quickly as from the New Testament: there is a charm about that book which draws forth the infant mind. But let us never be guilty, as parents, of forgetting the religious training of our children; for if we do we may be guilty of the blood of their souls.[5]

Forget Your Inhibitions

This is not a time to worry about your dignity. Role-play with your kids when they are small. Be Goliath, and give each of them a turn at being David. Have them throw a pillow or other object at you, then fall down when you get hit.

Act out Daniel in the lion's den. Be a lion and roar. Play out Bible stories with your children whenever you can. It will help them retain the principles behind the story.

If I remember correctly, when kids hear something, they retain 10 percent of what's heard. If they hear and *see* something, they retain about 40 percent. But if they actually *experience* something (see, hear, and participate in), they retain approximately 80 percent. (I can't remember the exact statistics, because I only heard them.)

Use the time when they are young and impressionable to impress upon them eternal biblical truths. I was deeply into role-playing until one memorable day: as I was rolling around on the floor doing something incredibly funny, I looked up and saw that none of my children were even cracking a smile. They were looking down at me as though I was some kind of nut. It was then that I realized they were no longer impressed. The "impressionable years" had gone.

Keep It Short...and Sweet

So the devotional time doesn't seem like a drag, don't make it too long. Keep it around 10 to 15, perhaps 20 minutes. In fact, if you stop devotions when the kids are having a good time, this will make them look forward to the next time.

From the Scripture passage you read, select a memory verse and have your kids repeat it together six times. Perhaps you could have them write memory verses in a special book, and review them regularly. Repeat the same verse each night during the week. If they remember it at the end of the week, give them some sort of reward (we often gave our kids a small amount of candy). The reward is important. We all need incentives in life, and candy is a good one.

In a moment you may think I own stock in Weight Watchers or in the dental industry. But I learned that children speak a special language called Candy, and if I wanted to communicate with them I could do so by speaking their language.

For years I ran successful kids' clubs, teaching the Bible to hundreds of children. If the kids learned a Bible verse, I would toss out candy as a reward. If they sat quietly and listened, I would toss out candy. If they even showed up, I would toss out candy. The kids loved it, and they kept coming back.

One time I told the three clubs that we were going to have a combined meeting, at which we would have "the world's biggest chocolate cake." I explained to a local bakery what I wanted to do, and they were very accommodating. I had friends carry in the huge cake like the Ark of the Covenant, and it caused about as much joy among those kids as the Ark would among adults.

So, be liberal when it comes to sweets. If you are worried about rotting your kids' teeth, have them brush after they have consumed their reward. If you are concerned about them becoming obese, make sure they eat only the candy you give them. And the reward doesn't have to be a big candy bar. A small bag containing a few jelly beans (the candy of presidents) can be just as rewarding to a child. This is for the most important of issues—their eternal salvation. So think about the fact that there will be plenty of healthy, fit, fine-teethed folks who will end up in hell.

My daughter's second child would not sit still for a moment. To say that she was active was a great understatement. Her parents, Rachel and EZ, were having a very frustrating time teaching her to read. They said she had my temperament, and I had to agree. I have super attention deficit disorder on steroids—I can hardly sit still for a moment. So I suggested that they give her incentives. My daughter smiled sweetly and said they didn't want to do that; Summer would simply have to learn self-discipline. After all, her elder sister was able to sit still and read for hours. I reminded Rachel that the child had my genes, and I knew that the way for me to motivate myself was with incentives.

That is what motivates me to write this book. My incentive is seeing you reading it, in my mind's eye. I imagine that you are sitting with your kids teaching them the things of God. I see them refusing the temptations of sex and drugs, because you have established a family altar and taught your children the fear of the Lord. I see them yielding their precious lives to the Savior and avoiding the damnation of eternal hell. I have the thought that perhaps I may play a small part in it by sharing simple life-changing, proven biblical principles. That is my "candy."

A few months after my suggestion, my daughter and son-in-law came to me and said, "We did what you suggested. We were pulling our hair out with frustration because Summer had the attention span of a flash bulb. She would not apply herself to learn. So we started giving her incentives, *and we can't believe the difference.* It's like night and day! She now loves to learn!"

I hope you aren't upset by my suggestion of using a little candy as a reward. I know some parents may have a problem with this, but perhaps you could find a substitute—a healthy treat or small monetary reward—and use that as an incentive instead.

Use Anecdotes and Humor

If you want to keep the attention of your children, thoroughly flavor the reading with anecdotes. It is said of the Messiah, "I will open my mouth in a parable" (Psalm 78:2). Jesus often used parables—stories that carried a deeper meaning. We must do the same.

A friend once told me of a doctor who had developed severe food poisoning. After he was taken to the emergency room he asked to see the EKG. He took one look at it and commented, "I'll be dead in fifteen minutes!" He was right. He had fifteen minutes to find peace with God. I hope he knew the way of salvation.

I heard about a woman who was in a serious car accident. As she lay dying in the hospital, she called for her mother, took her by the hand and said, "Mom, you taught me how to sew, how to cook, and how to keep house. You taught me everything about living, but you didn't teach me how to die!" How do you do that? How do you teach a child about death?

Sue and I went to the famed Knotts Berry Farm with my brother-in-law who loves roller-coasters. When he asked me to go on the insane "Montezuma's Revenge," I declined. This ride makes a complete 360-degree loop, goes part way up again, and then does the loop backwards!

As he walked through the gates alone, a feeling of sorrow for him clouded my good sense. I also felt embarrassed that my daughter, Rachel, had been on the ride five times. I gave up my battle with fear and joined him. When the ride ended, my knees were weak. I was consoled by the fact that the first time Rachel rode it she had been terrified too. The second time she was fearful, the third she was worried, the fourth ride she enjoyed, and by the fifth time she was bored. The more she experienced the ride, the less fearful she became. Instead of being paralyzed by fear, she learned to enjoy herself when she realized that there was nothing to fear. The roller-coaster had proven itself to be trustworthy.

That is the key to teaching your children about death. Why should we teach our children the Law and the "praises of the LORD, and His strength and His wonderful works that He has done" (Psalm 78:4)? Because they can learn from the experiences of men and women of God and likewise "set their hope in God, and...keep His commandments" (Psalm 78:7). Those who set their hope in God are free from the power and the fear of death.

You may not realize it, but I have just used three anecdotes:

- The man who had fifteen minutes to live

- The mother who taught her daughter about everything but dying

- The roller-coaster experience

Didn't they hold your interest? Follow in the steps of the greatest Teacher, and open your mouth in a parable. They will make your teaching more palatable. Make them short, and preferably humorous.[6]

Many people thank me for using humor when I teach, but occasionally someone will criticize this approach, asking me to justify it from a biblical perspective. One man wrote to say that "this is foolish jesting," which God aligns with "fornication, uncleanness, covetousness, and filthiness." This man began his serious letter by stating that Jesus didn't tell jokes, so we shouldn't either. Let me reprint my response to him, in the hope that it puts you at ease about making your kids laugh during your devotional times:

> Let me first say that I rarely use canned jokes (I'm not a joke-teller—I blow the punch-line). Jesus didn't

tell "jokes" either. But He did use witticisms ("strain out a gnat and swallow a camel," "I have married a wife, and therefore I cannot come," etc.). I do, however, use a certain type of humor in my sermons. It is usually putting myself down (dumb things I have done, or dumb things that have happened to me). Many years ago I did wonder if it was legitimate to use humor, and was delighted to find a quote by "The Prince of Preachers," Charles Spurgeon (my favorite preacher). He said that the use of humor in a sermon is like a flash of lightning on a dark night. It makes people sit up and wait for the next flash.

He also said that a famous preacher was once criticized because he made people laugh when he was speaking. "Yes," said Spurgeon, "was the wise answer, but did you not see that he made them cry directly after. That was good work, and it was well done." Then Spurgeon said of his own preaching, "I sometimes tickle my oyster until he opens his shell, and then I slip the knife in."

Airlines speak of the most sobering of subjects just before they take off—what to do if the plane is about to crash. Few people listen when they are giving (boring and predictable) emergency instructions. However, one employee-owned airline uses humor in its presentation, and it is amazing to see how everyone sits up and listens to the instructions.

Shortly after I wrote this letter, I spoke at a church. After the meeting, an excited woman approached me to say that her husband hadn't been to church for seven years, and that the last sermon he sat through was by what he called a "hell-fire" preacher. She added, "When you started, he said, 'Here we go again—another hell-fire preacher. I'm outta here.' But then you made him laugh, and he stayed for the whole sermon...and put his hand up at the end [indicating he made a commitment to Christ]."

Using humor in your family devotions will help serve as a gauge. Laughter not only reveals that your children are listening, but that they are congenial. But most important, humor keeps their attention so you can convey timeless truths.

The Phone Bird

The South Island of New Zealand doesn't have crows or mockingbirds. For our first year or so in the U.S., we were fascinated by the different birdcalls we heard in California. One day while working in the yard, I stopped to listen to the variety of songs. One in particular gripped my ears. It sounded very similar to a phone ringing. I stood there captivated by the sound, thinking, *I bet Californians call it a "phone bird." It sounds exactly like a phone ringing.*

Suddenly it dawned on me—it *was* the phone ringing! I missed the caller.

Notice that it was only when my understanding was right that the result was action. The night of my conversion, when my understanding was right, it resulted in action. My realization that I had sinned against a holy God led me to repent and place my faith in Jesus. "Faith comes by hearing [i.e., a right belief or understanding], and hearing by the word of God" (Romans 10:17). I know a lady who reads her Bible aloud because she believes that faith comes by literally hearing. However, I think it means more than that. As my own children heard the Word of God—and as they understood God's holiness, His justice, His truth, His righteousness, His love, and His faithfulness—they acted upon the Word by exercising saving faith, and came to know the salvation of God.

Now, commit yourself to having a family altar with your children. Do it as "a living sacrifice, holy, acceptable to God, which is your reasonable service" (Romans 12:1).

Remember to close the family devotions in prayer, asking God to help you and your family to remember—and act upon—the lessons you have learned.

A Family That Plays Together

It should go without saying that it's important to spend time with your children. This doesn't merely mean *quality* time. A "quality" hour in between weekly business trips can't be compared to *quantity* time. For a loving parent, this shouldn't be a sacrifice, but a highlight.

Over the years, I spent *many* hours with our kids up to my neck in a pond, trying to catch frogs. (In New Zealand there are no snakes, deadly spiders, or alligators.) We had our own frog pond in our yard, complete with a plastic diving board. The frogs loved it. We would put one on the end of the board, bend it down, and "twang" the frog into the air.

I would buy a roasted chicken, then the kids and I would stop in the woods on the way to our favorite pond and eat it "caveman style." Etiquette went out the door. These were some of the happiest moments of my life.

We also spent many hours playing football and other games. An avid tennis player once gave us about two dozen used tennis balls. Thanks to a tolerant wife and mother, the kids and I regularly upturned the furniture in our living room, split into two teams, put on protective plastic hats, and "bombed" each other with tennis balls. It was an absolute joy for me to live out my second childhood.

When Sue left for weekly meetings, we would dive at a recipe book, bake a cake, and eat it before she got back. However, times like this are more than just fun. They build a lifelong relationship between you and your children, so that they will love and respect you enough to trust what you say.

I feel sorry for parents who, as they were growing up, had a father who treated them like a dog with fleas. Didn't *their* fathers ever have fun with their own dads? Perhaps that was the problem. If that is your experience and you never had an intimate, fun-loving relationship with your dad, break the cycle. Get on your hands and knees and become a child again, for your children's sake.

A Family That Prays Together

Lastly, pray with your family every day. We referred to our prayer time as "T.O.P." (Time of Prayer). The moment I called out "T.O.P." the kids would stop what they were doing, and we would briefly pray together in the morning before we separated for the day. We would also pray after family devotions (each member would say a brief prayer), and Sue and I would pray heartfelt prayers of thanksgiving every night with the kids as we tucked them into bed.

In addition, Sue and I would have our own daily devotions together before we went to sleep, as well as our own separate personal time reading God's Word. This doesn't have to be for hours each day. All it takes is a few moments to honor the Lord and instill in your family the habit of daily time with God.

Spending time with your children—whether in learning, playing, or praying—is a great way to get to know them and lay a firm spiritual foundation. But to truly bring your children to Christ and keep them there, there is one more thing you need to know about them—an essential trait that you must be aware of. We'll look at this subject in the next chapter.

What a Lovely Child

MEN AND WOMEN tend to relate to babies differently (pass an infant to a man and see how awkward he looks), but one thing that both genders have in common when it comes to their offspring is something I call "ugly baby blindness." Face it, most newborns are a bit on the ugly side. But to the parents, the frog looks like a handsome prince.

One of the wonderful things about parenting is that it brings with it a blind love. This is important because the cute little infant is about to shake the very foundations of a peace-filled, happy marriage. The sweet, tiny babe is going to strip both parents of what they have taken for granted from the moment the marital knot was tied. He will steal sleep, peace, liberty, time, friendships, romance, intimacy, and even regular meals. He demands attention that leaves little room for much else. But love will carry the parents through.

Looking back on pictures of our newborns opened our eyes to love's blindness. Sue and I would stare in unbelief at old photos of our baby sparrows and say, "Man, we used to think they were gorgeous!" Blind love syndrome was never more evident than when friends would show us pictures of their baby sparrow, and use the word "cute" and "child" in the same sentence.

This built-in blind love, however, shouldn't be carried over to when the child begins doing ugly things. It is a tragedy when ugly behavior is seen as cute. One of the first horrible things to reveal itself in a child is the back arch. This usually appears when a parent uses the word "No," and stops the child from touching something. Mom or Dad then picks up the precious bundle and, instead of finding cuddly cuteness, is greeted with the back arch of protest.

This is the first sign of Syndrome Infantile Negative (SIN). It is rebellion against parental authority, and if it isn't dealt with, it will develop into a monster and affect everything in its path.

It shouldn't come as a shock to godly parents when this rebellion appears. They have seen it in their own hearts, so they know it is just a matter of time until it manifests in their darling offspring. At that point in life, a battle begins against the monster until it is destroyed.

Perhaps it makes you flinch to hear the word "monster" in reference to your beloved children, so let me back up my statements with Scripture; that way any argument you may have will be with God and not with me. Remember, don't let blind love stop you from seeing how ugly we all are, including your children. They have been born with the seed of Adam resident within, and if left to itself it will grow into a towering tree of evil. Here is how God describes our children's nature (from Romans 3:10–18):

They are not righteous in God's eyes. They don't understand or seek after God. If you leave them without godly instruction they will be destitute of true knowledge of their Creator. Like a magnet swings toward the north, human nature swings toward idolatry. They will turn aside and go the wrong way rather than the right way. They will choose darkness rather than light, evil rather than good. They have an inherent love of sin, which will become clearly evident when they hit the teenage years. The monster within them will want to be fed, and they will gladly yield to its appetite.

> Understandably, no parents like to consider their beloved children as evil, just as parents would reject any thought that their newborn is ugly.

Understandably, no parents like to consider their beloved children as evil, just as parents would reject any thought that their newborn is ugly. However, like the prodigal son, when a youth stretches his wings and gets away from the father's eye, sin is given full reign. If you listen to the conversation of typical godless teens, you will agree with the testimony of God that "their throat is an open tomb," and their mouths are "full of cursing and bitterness."

I'm sure it's difficult to picture the little child in your arms as having feet that are "swift to shed blood," but the potential to do so is there. Godless kids love violent movies and sadistic video games. They don't see the depictions of blood-thirsty murders as something horrific, but as entertainment to be enjoyed. It gives an adrenaline rush. This is why you must recognize the monster within your child and get rid of it at an early age. If it is not restrained, you can expect a lifetime of heartbreak.

Just Like Anybody Else

Many parents mistakenly look to a supposed goodness in the heart of their children to offer restraint. But man's "goodness" is a cracked dam that cannot restrain the force of sin. It is common for the mother of a vicious murderer to state that her teenage son was actually "a good boy." The mother of Scott Peterson, who was convicted in November 2004 of murdering his wife and unborn child, pleaded with jurors to "see the good in her son." Such loyalty is based on the unbiblical belief that there is good in everyone.

That's a common thought in today's society—that evil is something that's learned, not inherent, and that people are basically good. That thinking may seem to be true until you define the word "good." According to Scripture, it means to be morally excellent—to be perfect in thought, word, and deed. It means to love God with all of our heart, soul, mind, and strength, and to love our neighbor as much as we love ourselves. With that being the case, Jesus was right when He said that there is no one good except God (Mark 10:18).

So, reject the world's philosophy, and instead embrace the biblical viewpoint. Since God's Word says that there is *no one* good, your children, like the rest of us, aren't good—their hearts are evil.

Don't wait until you have a Jeffrey Dahmer on your hands before you use the word "evil" in relation to your children. That fiend murdered and cannibalized seventeen people, but his background is no different from that of most children. He himself said, "When I was a little kid I was just like anybody else."[7] However, when as a child he began showing cruelty to animals (something common in human nature), the monster wasn't restrained. So it is up to you to understand that the first back arch isn't cute; it's ugly. It is the beginning of rebellion and must be dealt with.

Perhaps the major reason children aren't corrected by their parents is that if parents refuse to acknowledge the reality of sin in their own lives, they won't acknowledge that evil dwells in the hearts of their offspring. They will justify their child's bad behavior by saying that he's basically a good kid because they don't see that his nature (like their own) is "desperately wicked" and urgently needs correction. We don't recognize evil because *we* are evil. It takes the light of God's Word to reveal the truth to us.

I live in Los Angeles County, and the city in which I live doesn't have a smog problem; all the other cities do. I can see the smog in the distance, hanging over them, but I can't see it in our city. However, if I get on a plane and fly over the entire area, I can see that a black poison covers every city in the county. It is from the higher altitude that I get a true perspective.

This is why we must rise above human reasoning to see God's perspective of good and evil. His Word tells us that "the heart is deceitful above all things, and desperately wicked" (Jeremiah 17:9). And if we have never believed the testimony of Scripture and seen the evil in our own wicked hearts, how will we ever see it in the hearts of our children? That's why it is essential to make sure that you are soundly saved yourself. Otherwise, you will be the blind leading the blind, and both you and your children will fall into the ditch of deception.

The Problem and the Cause

A television news story revealed that a well-known football player was having trouble with his memory. He would walk outside, remember that he had forgotten something, then go back in the house. By the time he got inside, he had forgotten what he went back for. This greatly concerned him. The story then mentioned that the player had received ten concussions in his football career. Slow-motion video clips showed him being tackled and violently hitting the ground.

At that moment I realized something I have never heard anyone mention. Although rugby, which is *very* popular in New Zealand, is as violent as football, there is one major difference. Americans are aghast that rugby players don't wear helmets or protective padding. Rugby players get bruised, they pull muscles, and they get bloody noses, yet concussions are reasonably rare. I have never heard of a player having *multiple* concussions, let alone ten!

I would suggest that the reason football players have concussions is that they wear protective helmets. Rugby players have an instinct to protect their heads when they tackle or fall. As they hit the ground, they instinctively hold their heads up. Football players, on the other hand, use their helmeted heads as battering rams. When they hit the ground, their head recoils, and the seven-pound helmet gives the head an even greater impact. I may be wrong, but it seems that *what they are trusting to protect their heads is the very thing that is causing the damage.*

This is the case with self-righteousness. Sinners are deceived into thinking that they are inherently good, and that their good works are pleasing in the sight of God. After all, how could doing good be bad? Their good deeds may be good for society, but they won't do them any good on the Day of Judgment. In fact, their good works have a bad result because the self-righteous don't see their need of a Savior. The very thing that they think is helping them is doing them eternal damage.

This is why it is so important to instill the Moral Law into young minds, before children learn to become self-righteous, to show them the standard of goodness that God requires. Its power, under the Holy Spirit, will help your children steer clear of the deception of self-righteousness, and bring them to the righteousness that is in Christ alone.

Consider Charles Spurgeon's instruction on how to bring children to the Savior—by being honest about their true nature:

> May our dear children know the cross, and they will have begun well. With all their gettings may they get an understanding of this, and they will have the foundation rightly laid.
>
> This will necessitate your teaching the child his need of a Savior. You must not hold back from this needful task. Do not flatter the child with delusive rubbish about his nature being good and needing to be developed. Tell him he must be born again. Don't bolster him up with the fancy of his own innocence, but show him his sin. Mention the childish sins to which he is prone, and pray the Holy Spirit to work conviction in his heart and conscience. Deal with the young in much the same way as you would with the old. Be thorough and honest with them. Flimsy religion is neither good for young nor old. These boys and girls need pardon through the precious blood as surely as any of us. Do not hesitate to tell the child his

ruin; he will not else desire the remedy. Tell him also of the punishment of sin, and warn him of its terror. Be tender, but be true. Do not hide from the youthful sinner the truth, however terrible it may be. Now that he has come to years of responsibility, if he believes not in Christ, it will go ill with him at the last great day. Set before him the judgment-seat, and remind him that he will have to give an account of things done in the body. Labor to arouse the conscience; and pray God the Holy Spirit to work by you till the heart becomes tender and the mind perceives the need of the great salvation.[8]

To help our children see God's perspective on goodness, we must first agree with His testimony about them being morally bankrupt—there is no one good, no, not one. Then we can rid them of the idea that their own righteousness will save them, by showing them the righteousness that God requires. In the following chapter, we'll look at a tool God has given us for this purpose.

Ally in Your Child's Heart

I ARRIVED IN Atlanta, Georgia, and made my way to my hotel. As I entered the room I tucked one of our Million Dollar Bill tracts[9] behind the door number. When my associate, Mark Spence, arrived later that night he would see the tract and know that he had the right room.

A few moments later I realized that I needed to replace a broken toothbrush, so I opened the door. Unbeknown to me, a hotel worker, carrying a tray of filled water glasses, had seen the tract. Because it looked like real money, she couldn't resist leaning the tray against the door in order to have a free hand to grab it. The moment the tray rested on the door was the very instant that I opened it. There was a big crash as glass broke and ice and water spread all over the floor.

I decided that my timing for opening the door was amazing, so perhaps God wanted me to share the gospel with this distressed woman. I spoke to her about her salvation, gave her a book, and told her that I would clean up the mess.

I spent the next several minutes down on the carpet searching for broken glass. Every time I thought I had picked up the last shard, however, I would see another one sparkle in the light.

In a similar way, sin lies hidden in the carpet of the human heart. Its sharp, bloodthirsty edge is concealed, undetected by the human eye. That's why we need the light of God's Law to detect it. Paul said he wasn't aware that sin hid in his heart, until the light of the Law had done its wonderful illuminating work (see Romans 7:7).

There are many biblical instances of the Moral Law being used to uncover sin. In Acts 28:23, the Bible tells us that Paul sought to persuade his hearers "concerning Jesus from both the Law of Moses and the prophets." Here we have two effective means of persuading the unsaved "concerning Jesus."

Let's first look at how the prophets can help persuade your children concerning Jesus. The Bible contains hundreds of prophecies foretelling the birth, life, death, and resurrection of the Messiah, as well as hundreds of other detailed prophecies that have been literally fulfilled. Since only an omniscient Being can know the future, fulfilled prophecy *proves* the inspiration of the Bible. So, familiarize yourself and your children with the prophetic words of

Isaiah, Ezekiel, Joel, etc.; the words of David in Psalm 22; of Jesus in Matthew 24 and Luke 21; and of Paul in 1 Timothy 4:1–5 and 2 Timothy 3:1–5. Show them that the Bible is no ordinary book but is truly the Word of God. It is also filled with incredible scientific facts, written in Scripture thousands of years before man "discovered" them.[10]

The other means by which Paul persuaded the lost was from "the law of Moses." Earlier I mentioned the use of the Moral Law to bring the knowledge of sin. It is essential that we not only understand it, but implement it.

The Bible tells us that the Law of Moses is good if it is used lawfully (1 Timothy 1:8). For what purpose was God's Law designed? The following verse tells us: "The Law is not made for a righteous person, but...for sinners" (v. 9). The Law

> The Law was designed primarily as an evangelistic tool—it was given by God as a "schoolmaster," or tutor, to bring us to Christ.

was designed primarily as an evangelistic tool—it was given by God as a "schoolmaster," or tutor, to bring us to Christ (Galatians 3:24). Paul wrote that "by the law is the knowledge of sin" (Romans 3:20).

The Law of God is obviously the "key of knowledge" Jesus mentioned in Luke 11:52. He was speaking to "lawyers"—those who were supposed to be teaching God's Law so that sinners would receive the "knowledge of sin," and thus recognize their need of the Savior.

Prophecy speaks to the *intellect*, while the Law speaks to the *conscience*. One produces *faith* in the Word of God; the other brings *knowledge* of sin in the heart of the sinner.

The Bible says in Psalm 19:7, "The law of the Lord is perfect converting the soul." Scripture makes it very clear that it is the Law that actually converts the soul. So many have missed this essential truth: the Moral Law is the God-given key that will unlock the door of salvation for your children. Because this concept may be new to you, please listen as Charles Spurgeon explains why the Law is necessary in salvation:

> It may be thought, by some people, to be a very sad thing that the Law should come into a man's heart to break it, and to cause him such sorrow and anguish as I am trying to describe. Ah, but it is not so; it is a very blessed thing. You cannot expect God to clothe you until he has stripped you, nor to heal you until he has cut the proud flesh out of your wounds. When a woman is sewing with a fine white silken thread, she must have a sharp needle to go first, to make a way for the thread to go through after it; and the anguish of spirit, which the Law creates in the soul, is just the sharp needle which makes a way for the fine silken thread of the gospel to enter our heart, and so to bless us. Let us thank God if ever we have experienced the entrance of

his Law into our hearts: for, although it makes sin to abound, it makes grace much more abound.

When the Law gets thoroughly into a man's heart, *it drives him to despair of himself.* "Oh!" says he, "I cannot keep that Law." Once, he thought that he was as good as other people, and a little better than most; and he did not know but that, with a little polishing, and a little help, he might be good enough, to win the favor of God and go to heaven; but when the Law entered his heart, it soon smashed his idol to atoms. The Dagon of self-righteousness speedily falls before the ten commands of God, and is so broken that it can never be mended. Men try to set the stump of it up on its pedestal again; but so long as the Law of the Lord is in the same temple with self-righteousness, self-righteousness can never be exalted again. To some people, it seems to be a dreadful thing to give a man such a bad opinion of himself, but, indeed, it is the greatest blessing that could come to him, for when he despairs of himself, he will fly to Christ to save him. When the last crust is gone from his cupboard, he will cry to the great Giver of the bread of life, whereof, if a man eat, he shall live for ever. You must starve the sinner's self-righteousness to make him willing to feed on Christ; and thus the very depths of his despair, when he thinks that he must be lost for ever, will only lead him, by God's abundant love, to a fuller appreciation of the heights of God's grace.[11]

The Way of the Master

If you study how Jesus evangelized in Mark 10:17–21, you will notice how different His approach was from that of modern evangelism. A young man *ran* to Him (he was earnest), *knelt* down (in humility), called Jesus "good," then asked how he could obtain eternal life. However, Jesus didn't preach the cross, speak of God's love, or lead this potential convert in a sinner's prayer. Instead He corrected the man's understanding of the word "good." Jesus took him through the Ten Commandments to show him God's standard of goodness, thereby exposing the man's hidden sin. This man had broken the First Commandment—his money was his god.

This is what we must do with our children. We need to imitate the way of the Master when it comes to dealing with *all* of the unsaved, including our family.

To check your child's understanding of salvation, ask if he thinks he is a good person. He will almost certainly say that he is, if he has no knowledge of sin (see Proverbs 20:6). This is because, without the Law, he has no understanding that in God's eyes "good" is moral perfection—in thought, word, and deed. Then go through the Ten Commandments, opening up their spiritual nature, and show that none of us can be good as far as God is concerned.

When we implement this incredible tool that Charles Spurgeon referred to as our most powerful weapon, we circumnavigate the human intellect and speak directly to the conscience. Scripture tells us that the human mind is at war with God, and is not subject to His Law (Romans 8:7). Therefore, to witness effectively, we have to find ground upon which there is agreement with the Law, so that we can reason with the lost about sin, righteousness, and judgment to come (John 16:8). That place of common ground is the conscience: "the work of the law [is] written in their hearts, their conscience also bearing witness..." (Romans 2:15).

Human understanding is "darkened" (Ephesians 4:18), but the conscience is the area where God has given light. The word *con-science* means "with knowledge." The conscience is the headline, written boldly to warn of sin, while the Scriptures give the fine print. None of us can say that we don't know it's wrong to lie, steal, murder, or commit adultery; that knowledge is written in large print on our heart. However, in the Scriptures we see the true nature of sin: that God requires truth even in the inward parts (see Psalm 51:6). The fine print reveals that lust is adultery of the heart, hatred is murder of the heart, fibs are bearing false witness, etc.

When you *reason* with your child about sin (what's in his heart), righteousness (which is of the Law), and judgment (eternal hell), simply say to him, "You *know* that it's wrong to steal, to lie, etc." As you do so, his conscience affirms within him the truth of the Law. You will more than likely notice that he subconsciously nods his head in agreement as you go through the Commandments.[12] The ally in his heart—his conscience—will side with you as you do so.

Following is a letter we received from a grateful mother who can attest to the effectiveness of the Law in appealing to the conscience:

> As I watched your show I was reminded that I had read Ray's book *Hell's Best Kept Secret* about a year and a half ago. I immediately went to your website and started going through everything that you had available. I ordered the "Foundation Course"[13] and then I downloaded the "Ten Commandments for Kids." My son, Hunter, is going to be five in June and is attending a Christian school and loves it, so I thought he would enjoy learning the Ten Commandments. I printed them out and we began. He had a great time going through each one. He even told me to remind him when he got older about "the adultery" one.
>
> When we got to the Ninth Commandment, he looked at me very seriously and said, "Mom, I broke that one!" He explained that he had told his dad and me a lie one day regarding a dream he had had about French fries. I told him that when he said his prayers that night he could ask the Lord to forgive him, and he agreed. That night as he was getting into bed I reminded him of the lie that he had told and

said now would be a good time to ask Jesus to forgive him. He was scared, to say the least, and he asked me to ask Jesus for him. I told him that he needed to do it for himself, but I offered to say the words and he could repeat them to Jesus. He agreed and I began to pray.

When we got to the part of asking forgiveness for his lie, Hunter started to cry. Then when he acknowledged that Jesus died on the cross to pay the penalty for his lie, he started howling! Here was my precious little boy in deep spiritual pain because he knew that Jesus had died because he told a lie about French fries! My son cried and howled in my arms for 45 minutes. After rocking him awhile, I explained that Jesus has forgiven him and is healing his heart right now of that sin. A little later I leaned over him to pull up his covers and Hunter said, "Be careful, Mom, you're squishing my heart. Jesus just healed it and I don't want it to break again!"

I was surprised the next day when he wanted to study the Ten Commandments some more. When we got to the Ninth Commandment, Hunter got a very somber expression, then looked at me intently. He said, "Mom, I'm really sorry about telling that lie!" I replied, "Hunter, you've been forgiven by the Lord for that and you don't need to worry about it ever again. It is forgotten! You now know how important it is not to sin, and you also know that if you do sin, you can go to Jesus and tell Him about it. If you ask Him to forgive you, He promises that He is faithful to forgive you! Isn't that great news?" He nodded in agreement.

Thank you for teaching me the importance of using the Law to uncover sin and to prick the conscience. I don't think my son will so easily tell a lie again...and neither will I! —*Donna W.*

Since God desires that all come to repentance, be sure to use the tools He has provided for that purpose. The conscience, your God-given ally in the hearts of your children, will work with you as you go through the Moral Law, convincing them of their need for a Savior.

In the next chapter, we'll explore further the concept of true and false conversion. To bring about the genuine salvation of your children, help them appreciate the cross so they come to Christ with the right motive.

Chapter Six

True and False Conversion

H AVE YOU EVER purchased something at a very low price and rejoiced about getting a bargain...right up until it broke? Then you realized that you should have purchased the more expensive but better quality item. Don't fall into the trap of doing the same thing with the salvation of your children. You don't want to cheapen the gift of God's grace, yet that's what will happen if your children don't understand sin in its true light. Neither do you want to lead them into a false conversion. To do so would be an unspeakable tragedy.

The Bible speaks plainly of false conversions many times, particularly in the Parable of the Sower (Matthew 13; Mark 4; Luke 8). Jesus referred to this category of people as "tares" among the wheat, "bad" fish among the good, "foolish virgins" among the wise, etc., and warned that on the Day of Judgment many would cry out, "Lord, Lord," and He would say to them, "I do not know you...Depart from Me, all you workers of iniquity" (Luke 13:27). The word "iniquity" means "lawlessness." These are professing Christians who have no concern when they transgress God's Law (the Ten Commandments). They don't keep their word. They take things that belong to other people. They don't guard their heart when it comes to lust. On Judgment Day, they will be found by God's Law to be lying, thieving, adulterers at heart. They will expect heaven, and instead find that they end up in hell. What a fearful thing to happen to anyone—*let alone your beloved children.*

So make sure that you understand the true nature of sin, and that you yourself have repented and been genuinely saved. The double tragedy with false converts is that they are deceived into thinking that they are saved, when they aren't. The Bible cautions us to "examine" ourselves to see if we are in the faith (2 Corinthians 13:5).[14]

As I mentioned earlier, I frequently receive letters from distraught parents who say something like this: "Johnny gave his heart to Jesus when he was four, but now that he's grown up, he's on drugs and living with his girlfriend." In Luke 9:62, Jesus warned that if we even "look" back from following Him, we are not fit for the kingdom. Those who fall away don't just *look* back, they *go* back. So something is clearly wrong when a child strays from the things of God. It is therefore essential that we understand about the pitfalls of steering our beloved offspring into a false conversion.

Leading a child in what is commonly called a "sinner's prayer," when there is no understanding of the true nature of sin, can do great damage. Consider this letter from a very (rightfully) concerned mother:

> It was at a youth camp that my oldest son "gave his heart to Jesus" and was baptized, but since then has shown no real desire that I can see to live for the Lord. I don't want to seem critical, but I just don't see the desire in any way, shape, or form. I don't want to see the same thing happen with my other two kids.

God only knows how many others have had the experience of seeing false professions of faith from loved ones. When these false converts fall away, they become bitter, and their latter end becomes *worse* than the first (see 2 Peter 2:20). They are inoculated against the truth.

When we teach children that salvation is as simple as saying a prayer, it often results in the terrible tragedy of a teenager being "gospel hardened." He thinks he "tried Jesus" when he was a kid, and it didn't work. It also reveals shallow theology on our part. It is an absolute necessity for the Holy Spirit to bring conviction of sin, because if there is no conviction of sin, there cannot be any repentance from sin. And without repentance there can be no salvation. Although we may work with the Holy Spirit, salvation isn't something we can in any way manipulate or create.

The way to work with the Holy Spirit is to use the Ten Commandments to bring "the knowledge of sin." Your children will never appreciate the cross until they understand the demands of the Moral Law. Why on earth did Jesus die? It was primarily to fulfill the demands of the Law (Matthew 5:17).

Going for the Jugular

The temptation for us as parents is to tell our children to come to Christ because He's their friend and will always be there for their every problem. All they need to do is talk to Him in prayer when they have a problem, and God will provide the answer. While this is true, there is one big qualification. Consider this analogy.

A child was once running through a wooded area when he fell onto a sharp stick and pierced his jugular vein. His father immediately scooped him up, held his thumb on the child's bleeding neck, and rushed him to a nearby hospital.

As they burst into the emergency room and a surgeon approached them, the small boy lifted his hand. When he fell, a tiny splinter had penetrated his thumb and he wanted the doctor to take it out. Of course, the good doctor ignored the child's plea, and immediately began work to stop the life-threatening injury to his neck.

In its ignorance, modern evangelism (as opposed to *biblical* evangelism) preaches a message that causes the sinner to hold up his splintered thumb to God, rather than that which is truly life-threatening. It tells the world that Jesus will fix the splinter of a bad marriage, drug addiction, alcoholism, loneliness, etc., when the *real* reason a sinner should come to the Savior is that his life's blood is draining from his neck. God wants to first deal with the fatal wound of sin—our spiritual problem—before He even looks at the splinter of our temporal problems.

The fact of sin is an eternal issue. The problems of this life, painful though they may be, are merely temporary. This is why it is important not to fall into the trap of modern evangelism's methods. It is easy to bring our children to a "decision for Christ" by telling them that Jesus will help them through life. But when we paint a pleasant picture of God as our children's friend, we fall into this trap.

The reality is that they are not God's friends, but His enemies, and are under His wrath because of their sin (Romans 5:9,10). This thought is perhaps contrary to what you yourself have been taught to believe. But think of this— how can children find a place of biblical repentance before the God they have offended (angered), if all they have been led to believe is that they have His jovial smile? What then do we tell them about God?

What we should be telling our children is that without the righteousness of Christ, they will perish on the day of wrath. And there is a way to do it without terrorizing them.

Recently, two boys who were fishing tried to cross a swift stream. As they did so, a log knocked them both into deeper water. One made it to the riverbank but the other got into difficulty. A man saw him and dived in, and after a long while fighting the current, he finally got the boy to the edge of the riverbank. Lifting the lad with both arms, he tossed him onto the bank. A woman grabbed the boy, and watched as the exhausted man sank down into the water. He came up once more, and then drowned. Tragically, he gave his all in saving the boy, and had nothing left with which to save himself.

Imagine relating the ending of that story to someone without giving the details preceding it: "A man drowned in a river today." The truth is that the danger the boy was in, due to the swiftness of the current, led the man to give his all, showing what concern he had for the child.

Don't merely tell your kids, "Jesus died for you on the cross." Teach them the reality of sin. The swift current of Eternal Justice was sweeping all of humanity into the very jaws of hell, but Jesus gave His all to redeem us from the curse of the Law, being made a curse for us. Teach the Law to your children and you will help them appreciate what Christ did for them on the cross.

Getting Tired

I ride a bike to work each day. It's only half a mile, but it keeps me fit. Sometime ago, however, I felt as though I was in my late nineties when I arrived at the ministry each day. I was exhausted. So I decided to pump up my bicycle tires. What a difference! I suddenly felt as though I were in my teens.

How do you get your kids pumped about the things of God? How do you get them in a place where their Christian walk is a great joy to them? It is by teaching them the Ten Commandments. If you skip the Law and instead tell them about the wonders of the cross, you may do them a great disservice. This is why: The Bible tells us, "To whom little is forgiven, the same loves little" (Luke 7:47). If you want your children to love the Lord with all of their heart, then allow them the joy of seeing what a great debt they have been forgiven in the cross.

The way to do that is to go back to the Law. If they are taught through the Law how exceedingly sinful sin is in the sight of God (Romans 7:13)—if they realize that they deserve eternal punishment—then they will begin to understand what God did for them through Christ. I had no understanding of the cross whatsoever until I learned that God saw my lust as adultery and hatred as murder. It is the knowledge of what I have been forgiven of (and what I have avoided) that makes me love the Lord with all of my heart.

Consider the following letter we received regarding this issue:

> The Lord graciously led us to one of "The Way of the Master" programs on TV. We were so excited to hear this message, we went to the website and listened to "True and False Conversion."[15] It was incredible. I had been very concerned in particular about our old-

est son, Isaiah, who had made a profession of faith about a year ago but I hadn't seen evidence/fruit of true repentance. When I heard "True and False Conversion," I realized that he hadn't truly repented. The Lord led me to begin talking with my son about the fruit of the Spirit versus the works of the flesh. He was clearly convicted. From there, I went into the Law.

Twice Isaiah was so broken he tried to run out of the room. He cried so hard he almost fell out of his chair. I have *never* seen anything like it before in my life (I've been saved for 10 years). When we went from judgment to the "foot of the blood-stained cross," his entire demeanor changed. Broken and without hope, he reached for our blessed Savior! And I was right there when my baby was saved from hell!

I cannot express to you my gratitude for the Lord's hand upon your ministry. I have observed little buds of fruit in him. The most beautiful fruit is his tears now for the lost and his desire to share Christ with others. He was so hardhearted before! —*Adrienne L.*

Here is another letter from a grateful teenager:

I can't even begin to thank you enough for your ministry. I am sixteen years old, and I love all of your tracts, books, and videos. I had been reading *Revival's Golden Key*,[16] and was sitting at the computer reading one of your columns. My eyes filled with tears as I realized that I wasn't truly saved! I had grown up in a

Christian home, I witnessed every week, I taught all kinds of classes, I did every Christian thing possible, but I had never been brought to salvation through the Law. I guess I never really wanted to examine myself and face the facts. The funny thing is, it was on April 1st, 2004, that I truly prayed for forgiveness—April Fool's Day. I had only been fooling myself! Thank you, thank you, and thank you!

> The key in bringing any person to the cross in true repentance is to use the Ten Commandments (God's Moral Law) to show him his need.

I am now trying to live my life to please God, out of gratitude! God has softened my heart, and has truly given me a compassion for those who are lost. I get so excited every time I see you preaching on video, or watching you witness. I want to do that! I can't wait to get out in this world and hand out tracts. Thank you from the very bottom of my heart! —*Jacqueline*

The Great Key

Because those who are forgiven much love much, those who are genuinely saved will bear the fruit of gratitude for the Lord and compassion for the lost. The key, then, in bringing any person to the cross in true repentance is to use the Ten Commandments (God's Moral Law) to show him his need. This is what Jesus did (e.g., Mark 10:17–21; Luke

18:18–22).[17] This is what Paul taught in the Book of Romans. It was the great key to the successful ministries of men such as Charles Spurgeon, John Wesley, and George Whitefield. According to Spurgeon, the Law is an essential part of the evangelistic message: "I do not believe that any man can preach the gospel who does not preach the Law." Unless sinners come to recognize the bad news of their guilt before a holy God, they will not understand the good news of the cross, and will not come to Christ for the right reason. Spurgeon warns,

> Lower the Law and you dim the light by which man perceives his guilt; this is a very serious loss to the sinner rather than a gain; for it lessens the likelihood of his conviction and conversion. I say you have deprived the gospel of its ablest auxiliary [its most powerful weapon] when you have set aside the Law. You have taken away from it the schoolmaster that is to bring men to Christ...They will never accept grace till they tremble before a just and holy Law. Therefore the Law serves a most necessary purpose, and it must not be removed from its place.[18]

In his book *Holiness*, J. C. Ryle writes of the sinner's motivation in coming to Christ:

> People will never set their faces decidedly towards heaven, and live like pilgrims, until they really feel that they are in danger of hell...Let us expound and

beat out the Ten Commandments, and show the length, and breadth, and depth, and height of their requirements. This is the way of our Lord in the Sermon on the Mount [Matthew 5:30]. We cannot do better than follow His plan.

We may depend on it: men will never come to Jesus, and stay with Jesus, and live for Jesus, unless they really know why they are to come, and what is their need. Those whom the Spirit draws to Jesus are those whom the Spirit has convinced of sin. Without thorough conviction of sin, men may seem to come to Jesus and follow Him for a season, but they will soon fall away and return to the world.[19]

Individuals who come to Christ in true conversion must first be convinced of their sin. Therefore, to bring your children to Christ—and keep them there—the Bible says to teach them the Law. Through Moses, God instructed the Israelites to teach the Law "diligently to your children" (Deuteronomy 6:7–9). He told them to talk with their children about the Commandments when they sit in their houses, when they walk with them, when they lie down, and when they get up. He said to bind it on their hands and in front of their eyes. He told them to put the Law upon the posts of their houses and on the gates.

Clearly, God wants our children to know the Ten Commandments—not to improve their memory or to help them win an Awana contest, but to awaken their conscience and prepare the soil of their hearts for the life-giving seed of the gospel. Look at Spurgeon's instruction to Sunday school teachers:

> I would have a Sunday school teacher watchful over the morals of the boys and girls under his care, speaking to them very particularly of those sins which are most common to youth. He may honestly and conveniently say many things to his children which no one else can say, especially when reminding them of the sin of lying, so common with children, or the sin of petty theft, or of disobedience to parents, or of breaking the Sabbath-day. I would have the teacher be very particular in mentioning these evils one by one; for it is of little avail talking to them about sins in the mass, you must take them one by one, just as David did.[20]

As Spurgeon alluded, mentioning sin in general—such as "All have sinned" (Romans 3:23)—typically fails to bring about the conviction of specific, personal sins. Then he suggests reminding children of the Moral Law, naming four of the Ten Commandments. In the next two chapters, we will follow his advice by going through the Ten Commandments, taking them "one by one."

The Mirror of the Law

L ET'S TAKE THE time to open up God's Moral Law and discover its power to bring the "knowledge of sin" (see Romans 3:19,20; 7:7), and reveal to our children their desperate need of the Savior. It would be wise for you to look into the mirror of the Law also (in doing so, a close friend of mine was transformed overnight by its power). As you go through the Commandments, not only judge yourself, but learn how to present them to others. I have included suggestions on how you can explain the Commandments to your children in a way they will understand.

First Place

The First Commandment, "You shall have no other gods before Me" (Exodus 20:3), requires that we put God first in our affections. That's not an option. Failure to obey this command implicitly is sin. Some may claim that they have always loved God, but the Bible says that there is none who

93

seeks God; we _all_ have gone astray, and "we have turned, _every one_, to his own way" (Romans 3:11; Isaiah 53:6).

Explain that Jesus said we should love God so much that all of our other affections—for our parents, siblings, and even our own life—should seem like hatred compared to the love we have for the God who gave our loved ones and our life to us (see Luke 14:26). It has been rightly said that if the greatest Commandment is to love God with all of our heart, soul, mind, and strength (see Mark 12:30), then the greatest sin is the failure to do so.

To help your children understand what this means, have them give you a toy or other small gift. Then pretend to love the gift more than you love the giver. Tell the giver to go away, because you want to spend time with the gift.

Explain that this is what we have done with God. He has showered us with gifts—giving us our life, freedom, food, family, eyes, ears, and a mind with which to think—and yet we love all these gifts while ignoring the Giver. We show what we truly love by how we spend our time and attention.

If someone gave us a valuable gift, such as an expensive new car, should we thank the person? Of course we should. God gave us life itself. Should we therefore be thankful to Him? Of course we should. We are infinitely indebted to God for the precious gift of life. So bring out these thoughts to instill in your children the fact that God doesn't owe us _anything_. Rather, we owe Him _everything_.

Ask your children what they have that wasn't given to them. Everything they have came through the goodness of God.

Have one of your children give you a candy bar and politely tell you, "I would like to give this to you." As it is being offered, reach out and snatch it, and don't say, "Thank you." Unwrap it and stuff it into your mouth, then (after you've swallowed) ask, "What's wrong with that?" Explain how sinful it is to be ungrateful. Teach your children that it is a sin to even eat a meal without being thankful to God.

Fast Food

If I am still on earth when the last trumpet sounds, I am going to need a new body—I will burst with sheer joy to know that it means an end to all the sufferings of this life. No more pain. No more fear. No more disease, dentists, decay, death, dandruff...and (praise the Lord) no more fasting! *Oh, how I hate fasting.* I have friends who can fast for several days and hardly notice, while I get hungry at the mere thought of missing a meal. I'm serious. When it comes to "spirituality," I am very shallow. With no fuel in this tank, I grind to a halt. I am normally happy and carefree, but if I miss food I lose my joy and get grumpy.

Yet, despite this weakness, I have fasted two meals a week for over thirty years. I don't say that to boast, because God knows how pathetic I have been over those years. I have sometimes had to break the fast and have tried many times to get out of it, but I have resigned myself that this is something I must do for my own good.

Even though I complain about missing meals, there are obvious benefits to fasting. One is that by skipping just two meals a week for thirty years, I have kept over a million calories from entering this little body of mine. If I had not practiced regular fasting I would probably have a built-in pulpit.

Another benefit is that it teaches me self-control. An appetite without self-control is like a fast car without brakes. In our godless world that spurns restraint, the lost want to live in the fast-food lane; brakes are for wimps. Because the self-indulgent want the freedom to eat anything anytime anywhere, obesity has become a huge problem in America. It's a bulging epidemic. Multitudes in the U.S. are diseased and dying because they don't control their appetites. Even the world is beginning to see this lack of control as a problem. In an article titled "The Power of No," *Newsweek* states:

> It's an unanticipated legacy of the affluent '90s: parents who can't or won't set limits. Now a growing number of psychologists are warning of the dangers of overindulgence and teaching how—and where—to draw the line.[21]

I wouldn't be considered a "health freak" by most people's standards. However, I am sometimes horrified at what I see Christians shovel into their mouths. It's not only the quantity that concerns me, it's the quality of food they consume. For years I have had an itinerant ministry, and have therefore shared a table with thousands of Christians. At times I have felt like saying, "Look at what you are eating! No wonder you are so overweight. If you keep going down that path, you will die prematurely." As Christians who love God and want to serve Him, we need to keep the body in running order, but that won't happen if we don't use wisdom in what we eat. When 2thies

It is the body's immune system that fights off disease. A strong immune system will better enable you to resist illness; a weak one makes you vulnerable to all sorts of ailments. Keeping this simple principle in mind will help you take better care of yourself as well as your children. How do you build up the immune system? Here's a rule of thumb: If God made it, it's good. If man made it, check the label. Give your kids plenty of fruits, vegetables, and nuts. Tell them why they should drink water rather than sodas. Water will purify their system; sodas will pollute it, and are full of sugar and chemicals. Explain to your children that they are the temple of the Holy Spirit, so they should respect the body that God has given to them. NEST.

Aside from the health aspects, another wonderful benefit of fasting is that it has given me gratitude for every meal I sit down to eat. I say grace before, during, and after each meal. Ask my wife. I get delirious with joy over a potential chicken (an egg). I love cereal and could swim through a swimming pool of milk with my mouth wide open. I am very thankful to God for giving us so much good food. Like the disciples, I eat my food with "gladness."

We don't truly appreciate many things in life until we are deprived of them, and we don't have any real appreciation for food until we feel the roar of an empty stomach. Therefore, invite your kids to join you in a brief fast every now and then, explaining your reasons for doing so. Then, when it's finished, let them say grace for the next meal.

When our kids were little, we played "blindfold" with them, challenging them to walk around blindfolded for one hour. That simple exercise not only enabled them to feel empathy for the blind, but it gave them gratitude for God-given eyesight.

Children left without godly instruction will take their health, food, eyesight, parents, and life itself for granted. Ask your children if they have ever been guilty of failing to put God first in their affections and praising Him for all that He has lavished upon them.

One True God

The Second Commandment is, "You shall not make for yourself any carved image" (Exodus 20:4).[22] This command means that we shouldn't make a god to suit ourselves, either with our hands or with our minds. Someone once said that God created man in His image, and man has been returning the favor ever since. Most of us are guilty of fashioning a god in our own image. Our god doesn't mind lust, or a fib here and there. He doesn't have any moral dictates. In truth, our god doesn't exist. He is a figment of our imagination, shaped to conform to our sins.

We are also guilty of idolatry when we picture God as a benevolent Santa Claus figure who dispenses good things and won't punish us for our sins, believing that He is too loving to send anyone to hell. But consider what the Bible reveals about our Creator. The Book of Genesis tells us that God killed a man because He didn't like his sexual activities. He commanded Joshua to kill every Canaanite man, woman, and child, without mercy. He drowned the whole human race, except for Noah and his family, in the Flood. He killed a man for merely touching the Ark of the Covenant. In the New Testament, He killed a husband and wife because they told one lie. That God is not so easy to snuggle up to.

Rather than wondering why God would kill a couple for telling a lie, we should ask, "Why didn't God kill *me* when I lied for the first time?" God simply treated them according to their sins. When we did wrong for the first time and didn't get struck by lightning, we concluded that God didn't see or didn't care about what we did. With our erroneous image of God, we became bolder in our sin. For that reason, idolatry is perhaps the greatest of sins because it allows us to engage in unrestrained evil.

If we caught a true revelation of our Creator, we would fall flat on our faces in terror. We tend to want to steer clear of these thoughts when it comes to teaching our children about God, but we should instead do the opposite, and instill in them a healthy fear of God.

Even though I didn't have a Christian upbringing, it was the fear of God that kept me from sinning against Him. I remember one night finding myself, at the age of sixteen, lying in long grass outside a dancehall with a pretty young girl. It was a dream come true for a red-blooded teenage male. I was about to make my move when she looked to the starry sky and sweetly said, "You know...God is watching us." I didn't say, "No, that's not true. God is limited in His presence. He can't see *everything*. Even if He did, He wouldn't punish me for any wrongdoing." Instead, the work of the Law that was written in my godless heart kicked in and did its duty. I immediately knew that God frowned on my intentions—a thought that was more powerful than a bucket of ice water. We got up and went back inside the dancehall.

As I look back, that incident could have saved two kids from a lifetime of regret. That's why it's crucial that we teach our children the character of the one true God who has revealed Himself in the Bible.

Drop the Egg

To help your children understand the nature of God and His Moral Law, talk to them about some of God's natural laws. Call your kids over to the refrigerator and take out an egg. Then, while they are watching, drop it onto the kitchen floor. I know what you are thinking: *I can't drop an egg on the floor!* Yes, you can; it's easy. Your children will forget the thousands of eggs that you carefully handled, but I am sure they will remember this one because it was *deliberately* dropped. Perhaps even in years to come, each time they take an egg from the refrigerator they will remember the valuable lesson they learned this day.

Maybe you are frugal, or you are a neat freak like me, but drop the egg anyway. It will be worth the cost and the mess (let the dog lick it up). Go on. Drop it. Let Humpty Dumpty fall.

Now ask your children why the egg broke. Ask what would happen to us if we jumped out of a plane without a parachute and landed on the ground. Many an optimistic, shallow-thinking skydiver has ended up like the egg on the floor, because he was foolish enough to toy with the invisible law of gravity. His cheap thrill cost him his life.

Explain the law of gravity to your kids. Look up "gravity" on the Internet or in a book, and then relate it to God as the Creator of the natural laws. Remind them of the fate of the egg, and let their eyes widen a little at the thought of transgressing its precepts.

The consequences for breaking gravitational or electrical laws are fearful. But they pale in the shadow of transgressing the eternal Moral Law of God. My feeble words can't express what God is like, but His Law gives us insight into His holy nature. The Law reveals utter holiness, supreme righteousness, and absolute truth. God has a terrifying and violent passion for justice. The Israelites were terrified when God spoke to them on Mount Sinai—and at the time He was merely giving them the Law, not revealing His anger when they broke its commands.

What has your own understanding of God been like? Do you tremble at the very thought of His power and holiness? Have you seen Him in the light of the Holy Scriptures, or have you made up a god to suit yourself? If it's the latter, then you are guilty of idolatry and you don't want to lead your children into the same fatal error. The Law's sentence for idolatry is death, and according to the Scriptures, no idolater will enter the kingdom of heaven (1 Corinthians 6:9,10). Ask your children if they have ever been guilty of this sin.

Above All Names

The Third Commandment is, "You shall not take the name of the LORD your God in vain" (Exodus 20:7). Have you ever given any thought to the origin of cuss words? It's rather strange. The words used to cuss may be quite an inoffensive part of the English language. Take for instance "damn" and "hell." The words in themselves have legitimate meanings. However, the manner in which they are used determines whether they fit into the category of cuss words.

Grab a hammer and pretend to hit your thumb with it. Ask your kids what you should say when pain explodes in your thumb. They will probably say, "Ouch!" Explain that some people may express anger at what happened by saying "cuss" words, or by using God's holy name. They are not actually angry at God for their pain; they just use His name in place of a filthy word to express disgust.

The Bible calls this blasphemy, and says that "the LORD will not hold him guiltless who takes His name in vain" (v. 7). Most people will say that they do this thoughtlessly, that the names of Almighty God and Jesus Christ—the name that is above all names—are just meaningless expressions to them. This strongly reinforces the Bible's claim that humanity hates God without cause (John 15:25). If you teach your children that unregenerate humanity hates God, then, if they ever hear blasphemy, what you have said will make sense.

> The Law reveals utter holiness, supreme righteousness, and absolute truth. God has a terrifying and violent passion for justice.

What greater contempt can you have for an enemy than to use his name to curse? To slur someone's name is to insult the very person. God's name is synonymous with His character, so to use His name as profanity is to show contempt

103

Lord God forgive me please His convict neoztws [handwritten marginalia]

for who He is. Even Hitler's name wasn't despised enough to be used as a cuss word, yet people regularly take the name of the God who gave them life and drag it through the mud.

Ask your children if they have ever been guilty of this sin.

One in Seven

The Fourth Commandment tells us, "Remember the Sabbath day, to keep it holy"(Exodus 20:8). I ignored this command for twenty-two years of my non-Christian life. Never for a second did I say, "God gave me life; what does He therefore require of me?" Nor did I set aside one day in seven to rest and to worship Him in spirit and in truth.

Gather seven pieces of candy, and explain to your kids that all seven belong to you. It's *your* candy. Then put one on a plate and tell one of your children that it's now his, and that you are giving it to him because you love him. Don't let him eat it; just tell him that it's his. Then give him another. Put all seven on the plate one at a time and push the plate toward him, saying, "It's all yours. I am giving you all of them because I love you." Pause before asking, *"May I have one piece of candy back?"*

Tell him that it's only right that he should give you one in seven, if you ask him to. Then explain how God has served up seven days on a plate, and that it's only right that we give Him back one in seven, because that's what He has asked. State that it's human nature to want to keep all seven for ourselves, and that the Commandments reveal our sinful hearts. Ask your children if they have ever been guilty of the sin of refusing to give God what He asks.

Remember, the Ten Commandments were given not for justification, but to bring the knowledge of sin—to reveal how far we have fallen short of doing what we should. But once we come to Christ, we should follow the example of the early Church and gather for fellowship on the first day of the week (see "Freedom from Sabbath-keeping" in *The Evidence Bible*).

Obey Parents

The Fifth Commandment is, "Honor your father and your mother" (Exodus 20:12). Parents are to be valued implicitly, in a way that is pleasing in the sight of God. To honor parents is to esteem them, show them respect, and obey them. The Scriptures command children to "obey your parents in all things, for this is well pleasing to the Lord" (Colossians 3:20). This doesn't mean parents will always make perfect decisions, but that the children are still to honor and obey; that is the role for which God will hold them accountable.

As the first authority figures in a child's life, parents are God's agents to train (and discipline) the child in the ways of the Lord. A rebellious child who will not submit to his parents' authority and obey their rules is unlikely to grow up to submit to God's authority over his life and obey His Laws.

Don't hesitate to show your children God's instructions to Moses that if a rebellious youth was continually disobedient, he was to be stoned to death: WOW

> If a man has a stubborn and rebellious son who will not obey the voice of his father or the voice of his mother, and who, when they have chastened him, will not heed them, then his father and his mother shall take hold of him and bring him out to the elders of his city, to the gate of his city. And they shall say to the elders of his city, "This son of ours is stubborn and rebellious; he will not obey our voice; he is a glutton and a drunkard." Then all the men of his city shall stone him to death with stones; so you shall put away the evil from among you, and all Israel shall hear and fear. (Deuteronomy 21:18–21)

Scripture records one occurrence of a child actually being stoned to death. In Leviticus 24:11–23, a disobedient son is stoned for blaspheming the name of the LORD. Can you imagine any child in his right mind allowing rebellion to enter his heart, knowing that this terrible fate could be his? By teaching your children to be obedient, you will help them learn to have a healthy respect for both God's Law and man's.

Teaching respect within the home will also instill within your children a deep respect for *all* authority as they go through life, as well as respect for all people. Our kids knew that they were never to say "No" in a rebellious way to their parents. When one of my boys was about eleven years old, he walked through the doorway in front of his mother. I gave him a *very* firm tap on his shoulder and made sure he understood that he was never to treat any woman with such a lack of respect. He has never done it since, and he now treats his wife with the utmost respect.

Sticker Shock

If possible, gather photos of your children at their birth, and perhaps pictures of their mother while she was pregnant. Talk with your kids about the realities of morning sickness, the pain of childbirth, the countless nights of lost sleep because of a crying baby, etc. Help them to see the loving sacrifices involved in parenting.

If your kids are old enough, have each of them guess how much it costs parents to raise a child until he leaves home and gets married. Offer a dollar bill to the child who guesses the closest (then add one more dollar to your total). Using a calculator, work with them to show the cost of raising a child—food, clothing, housing, utilities, insurance, transportation, education, etc. When you get a total (it will probably shock you), tell them that it is your joy to take care of them because you love them so much. Then ask what attitude kids should have toward their loving parents.

Ask if they have *always* honored their parents in a way that is pleasing in God's sight. Have they always had a perfect attitude in all things toward you? Encourage them to ask God to remind them of their hidden sins and wrongful attitudes. Then read and explain the following passage, and help them memorize it:

> Children, obey your parents in the Lord, for this is right. "Honor your father and mother," which is the first commandment with promise: "that it may be well with you and you may live long on the earth." (Ephesians 6:1–3)

Ask your children what they value most. The most precious thing they have is their life. Explain that as they grow up, their money, car, possessions, and other items are all useless if they lose their life. Like everyone else, they will want to enjoy a long life and have everything go well for them. Yet in this passage in Ephesians God promises that if they don't honor their parents, they will have neither.

Children who heed their parents' biblical training will find both:

> My son, give attention to my words; incline your ear to my sayings. Do not let them depart from your eyes; keep them in the midst of your heart; for they are life to those who find them, and health to all their flesh. (Proverbs 4:20–22)

A Terrible Disease

PERHAPS YOU ARE feeling uncomfortable about going through the Ten Commandments with your kids. The world would have you believe that the worst thing you could do for your children is to give them a sense of guilt. *But that is what you must do.* In doing so you are preparing their heart for gratitude for the cross. Your children, like all human beings, are guilty of breaking God's Moral Laws, and therefore *should* have a sense of guilt. It is this guilt that will drive them to the Savior. You are simply showing them that they have a terrible disease—the fatal disease of sin— so that they will want to seek the cure. Therefore, don't hold back in using God's Law to gently point out the symptoms.

Charles Spurgeon exhorts parents and teachers not to hold back the truth:

> Do not spare your child; let him know what sin leads to. Do not, like some people, be afraid of speaking plainly and broadly concerning the consequences

of sin. I have heard of a father, one of whose sons, a very ungodly young man, was taken off in a very sudden manner. The father did not, as some would have done, say to his family, "We hope your brother has gone to heaven." No; but overcoming his natural feelings, he was enabled by Divine grace to assemble his children together, and to say to them, "My sons and daughters, your brother is dead; I fear he is in hell. You knew his life and conduct, you saw how he behaved; and now God has snatched him away in his sins."

Then he solemnly told them of the place of woe to which he believed—yes, almost knew—he was gone, begging them to shun it, and to flee from the wrath to come. Thus he was the means of bringing his children to serious thought; but had he acted, as some would have done, with tenderness of heart, but not with honesty of purpose and said he hoped his son had gone to heaven, what would the other children have said? "If he is gone to heaven, there is no need for us to fear; we may live as we like." No, no; I hold that it is not un-Christian to say of some men that they are gone to hell, when we have seen that their lives have been hellish lives.

But it is asked, "Can you judge your fellow creatures?" No, but I can know them by their fruits. I do not judge them, or condemn them; they judge themselves. I have seen their sins go beforehand to judgment, and I do not doubt that they shall follow after.

"But may they not be saved at the eleventh hour?" I have heard of one who was, but I do not know that there ever was another, and I cannot tell that there ever will be.

Be honest, then, with your children and teach them, by the help of God, that "evil shall slay the wicked."[23]

Life Is Precious

The Sixth Commandment is, "You shall not murder" (Exodus 20:13). God, the Creator of life, commands us, "Do not shed innocent blood" (Jeremiah 7:6). Because human life is very precious, the Bible says that anyone who deliberately takes a life should lose his own: "Whoever sheds man's blood, by man his blood shall be shed; for in the image of God He made man" (Genesis 9:6). The seriousness of a crime is reflected in the punishment, so this shows the value God places on human life.

Once you have established what a terrible thing murder is, explain that, while few of us will actually take the life of another, that doesn't let us off the hook with this Commandment. God's Law is spiritual in nature, as Jesus showed. Read Matthew 5:21,22, in which Jesus warned that if we get angry without cause, we are in danger of judgment. In addition, if we hate someone, God considers us murderers (see 1 John 3:15). There are many who would like to kill, but who refrain out of fear of punishment. Because God sees their thought-life, He counts them guilty of committing the crime. We can violate the *spirit* of the Law by our attitude and intent.

If your children are mature enough, you may want to touch on the subject of abortion, explaining that civil law may smile on such a wicked crime, but God's Law does not. The Bible informs us that taking the life of the unborn is clearly murder: "He did not kill me from the womb, that my mother might have been my grave" (Jeremiah 20:17). God calls abortion murder, and the Bible says that no murderer has eternal life dwelling in him (1 John 3:15).

Sex Only Within Marriage

The Seventh Commandment is, "You shall not commit adultery." How do you discuss this topic with your children? Perhaps, like me, you find it very difficult to talk to kids about sex. One evening during family devotions, I read ahead in our Scripture passage and saw these verses:

> Let your fountain be blessed, and rejoice with the wife of your youth. As a loving deer and a graceful doe, let her breasts satisfy you at all times; and always be enraptured with her love. For why should you, my son, be enraptured by an immoral woman, and be embraced in the arms of a seductress? (Proverbs 5:18–20)

Our practice was to have each person in the family read a verse. I thought it would be easier for one of the kids to read the embarrassing portion, so I decided to simply pass the buck to one of them. But I made the mistake of *asking* my son, rather than telling him. I said, "Jacob, do you want to read the next verse?" To my shock, he answered, "No." So I casually asked, "Rachel, do you want to read the next verse?" She also said, "No." My youngest, Daniel, couldn't yet read, so I turned to my faithful wife for support. She gently but firmly shook her head. I realized where the buck had stopped, and ended up reading that passage of Scripture.

There was a reason for my reluctance: I suffer from Smirkinson's disease. The evident symptom of this embarrassing ailment is that my mouth turns up at the edges when I talk to kids about sex. I remember speaking to Jacob when he was in first grade. At that time he was attending a secular school, so I nonchalantly inquired, "Do kids talk about sex in school?" To my dismay, he said that they did—and he was only six years old!

> I suffer from Smirkinson's disease. The evident symptom of this embarrassing ailment is that my mouth turns up at the edges when I talk to kids about sex.

I left the room and had a conference with Sue in the hallway. We quickly concluded that I needed to have "the talk" with Jacob about the birds and the bees then and there.

I gathered my courage and walked back into the room, but was forced to do a U-turn into the hallway as symptoms of Smirkinson's manifested themselves on my face. Three times I had to do a U-turn before I was able (with Sue's encouragement) to stave off the symptoms and talk to my son about the delicate subject of sex.

So, with that dilemma in mind, let's look at how we can, without embarrassment, talk to our children about the sensitive subject of illicit sex—the issue of adultery.

Simply explain, "The Seventh Commandment says, 'You shall not commit adultery.' That means you should only sleep with the person to whom you are married." Kids are usually happy with the "sleeping together" explanation; you don't need to even mention the word "sex." Tell them that Jesus said if you even *want* to go to bed with someone else (which is called lust), you commit adultery with that person in your heart.

After watching our television program, "The Way of the Master," my six-year-old granddaughter asked her dad, "Why does Grandpa say every week, 'Whoever looks at a woman and lusts after her has already committed adultery with her in his heart'? He says it every time. What does it mean to lust?" My son-in-law discreetly explained that it means a man should not look at another woman in the way he looks at his wife. He shares a bed with her and shouldn't desire to share his bed with any other woman. He then added that when she was older, he would give her more details. She was satisfied with that answer.

In Matthew 5:27,28, Jesus again points out the spiritual nature of the Commandments. Even if we don't violate the letter of the Law, we can violate the *spirit* of the Law in our hearts. Help your children memorize Jesus' words:

> "You have heard that it was said to those of old, 'You shall not commit adultery.' But I say to you that whoever looks at a woman to lust for her has already committed adultery with her in his heart." (Matthew 5:27,28)

Review that verse often. One day your child might find himself in tall grass at night with an attractive member of the opposite sex, and that ice-water verse tucked into his heart may keep him from sexual sin—"Your word I have hidden in my heart, that I might not sin against You" (Psalm 119:11).

Instill in your children that God has seen every sin that every single person has ever committed. He has seen the deepest thoughts and desires of each of our hearts. Nothing is hidden from His pure eyes. The day will come when we will have to face the Judge whose Laws we have broken. The Scriptures say that the impure (those who are not pure in heart), the immoral (fornicators—those who have sex before marriage), and adulterers will not enter the kingdom of God (1 Corinthians 6:9,10).

Cleaning the Dog's Teeth

Buy a child's toothbrush, and gather some plain white wrapping paper and scotch tape. Remove the toothbrush from its packaging and clean your dog's teeth with it. Then take the smelly brush and your kids into your garage, and find a dirty corner. Clean the corner using the toothbrush. Scrub the sole of your shoe with it, and the wheels of your car. Make sure the brush is really filthy.

Now go back inside and carefully repackage the toothbrush and gift-wrap it in the nice white paper. Give it to one of your children, explaining that it is a special gift for him, and is the toothbrush he is to use from now on. Hopefully, your kids will be disgusted.

> Tell your kids that if God can create an ear, He can therefore hear everything they say. If He can create an eye, He can see everything they do.

Explain that the Bible depicts marriage as a picture of the relationship between Christ and the Church. He is the Groom and the Church is the bride for whom He is coming back one day (see Ephesians 5:31,32; 2 Corinthians 11:2).

The reason a bride wears a white wedding dress is to signify her purity (moral cleanness). Yet when people sleep with others and then meet the one they want to marry, it's as though they are offering their spouse a filthy toothbrush wrapped in nice white paper. They have been "used" by strangers for that which isn't lawful—taking what could lawfully be theirs as a gift from God, and corrupting it. This is like a child who one night steals a crisp, new twenty-dollar bill from his father's wallet, not realizing that his father intended to give it to him as a gift in the morning.

Tell your kids to keep themselves pure for the one God has for them to marry. And don't forget to ask as they near their teens, "Have you ever broken this Commandment?" (in thought or in deed).

"Stop, Thief!"

The Eighth Commandment is, "You shall not steal" (Exodus 20:15). Remind your children that God sees everything, and that He will judge us for everything we do (Ecclesiastes 12:14). Have them memorize Psalm 94:7–10:

> Yet they say, "The LORD does not see, nor does the God of Jacob understand." Understand, you senseless among the people; and you fools, when will you be wise? He who planted the ear, shall He not hear? He who formed the eye, shall He not see? He who instructs the nations, shall He not correct, He who teaches man knowledge?

Tell your kids that if God can create an ear, He can therefore hear everything they say. If He can create an eye,

He can see everything they do. If they have stolen even one item, then they are thieves, and God has seen their crime. The Bible tells us that no thief will enter heaven (1 Corinthians 6;9,10).

Open Your Wallet

Place twenty one-dollar bills into your spouse's purse or wallet. Pretend that it belongs to someone else as you open it, and instruct your kids to call out "Thief!" and point at you if they see you steal anything.

First, take out *all* the money. After your kids have yelled, "Thief!" put the money back into the wallet or purse, and this time take out only one dollar. More than likely they will call out "Thief!" with as much enthusiasm as when you took out all twenty dollars. The point is that God isn't concerned with the value of what is stolen. Theft is theft, regardless of the amount taken. Point out that theft can also include stealing an answer from someone else's test, bringing supplies home from school or a workplace, "borrowing" an item without permission, and so on.

Discuss with your kids whether it would be considered "stealing" if they were undercharged when buying something, or if they were given too much change, and they're aware of it. What's the honest thing to do in these situations? Help them see that both cases involve taking (or receiving) something that they know isn't rightfully theirs. Remind them that God requires truth in the inward parts.

Ask your children if they have ever taken something that didn't belong to them. If they have, say, "Then you are a thief, and you cannot enter heaven. The Bible warns that you will go to hell."

Don't be afraid to talk about hell with your children. The day will come when the lost will wish that believers had said much more to warn them. Sadly, sinners mention hell in their daily speech far more than the average Christian. Their language includes such phrases as: hell will freeze over, as sure as hell, give 'em hell, hell of a time, come hell or high water, hell's bells, as hot as hell, there will be hell to pay, etc.

Nothing But the Truth

The Ninth Commandment is, "You shall not bear false witness" (Exodus 20:16). Ask your children if they have ever told a fib, a "white lie," a half-truth, or an exaggeration. If they have, tell them that they have lied. Then ask, "How many lies do you have to tell to be a liar?" Telling just one lie will make them a liar.

In a 2004 survey of 20,000 teens, 82 percent admitted lying to their parents in the last year, yet 92 percent said they were satisfied with their ethics![24] Don't simply teach your children that lying is wrong; help them see how God views the sin. The Bible tells us, "Lying lips are extremely disgusting and hateful to the Lord..." (Proverbs 12:22, Amplified). Teach them that *all* sin is an offense to Him.

We may not think that deceitfulness is a serious sin, but God does. The Bible warns,

> All liars shall have their part in the lake which burns with fire and brimstone. (Revelation 21:8)

Don't be afraid to use the motive of fear to keep your kids from sin. Years ago, a television advertisement had a deep-voiced commentator ask a sobering question: "What goes through the mind of a driver at the moment of impact in a head-on collision if he's not wearing a seatbelt?" As he spoke, the ad showed a dummy without a safety belt reacting in slow motion to a head-on collision. As the dummy moved forward on impact, the steering wheel went right through its skull. Then the commentator somberly continued, "...the steering wheel. You can learn a lot from a dummy. Buckle up!"

Although the ad uses fear, it is a *legitimate* use because it *is* a fearful thing to have a steering wheel crush your head. So let your kids know that it is a fearful thing to fall into the hands of the living God (Hebrews 10:31).

Crooked Rivers

If possible, locate an aerial photograph of a river that meanders over the countryside. Explain to your children that rivers are often crooked because water takes the path of least resistance. That's the same reason men are crooked—they lie to take the easy path. Give your kids this example:

"Let's pretend that Tommy hit his sister. When his dad asks him if he hit his sister, he answers, 'No.' Tommy is telling a lie. Why do you think he is lying?" Bring out the fact that, like the river, Tommy is trying to take the easy path. He doesn't want to suffer the consequences of his sin.

Ask the kids to think about which commandments Tommy is breaking when he lies. In addition to lying (ninth), he's dishonoring his father (fifth); he's not putting God first (first); and he's showing that he doesn't have a proper fear of God (second). He is also demonstrating that he doesn't love his sister as himself, which is the essence of the Law (see Galatians 5:14).

As you teach your kids about honesty, they may ask, "You mean that if some lady asks me if I like her hat, I have to tell her the truth—that it's ugly?" Explain that there is a big difference between discretion (wise self-restraint in speech) and lying (a false statement intended to deceive), and that God knows the difference.

A Broken Tooth

Have you ever told someone that you would pray about a particular thing, and the person later thanks you for praying—and you suddenly realize that you forgot to pray? It's not a good feeling. So when I say that I will pray for someone I usually do it then and there, and I also try to remember to pray at the correct time.

The Bible says that placing your confidence in someone who doesn't keep his word is like having a bad tooth or a foot out of joint. They cause pain when you rely on them. I am frustrated by people who don't keep their word, so I try to avoid having any dealings with them. Thankfully, I am surrounded by faithful men and women, who, when they say they will do something, do it. And they do it on time.

You can usually tell an unfaithful person (a liar) by what comes out of his mouth. He will say, "I *promise* to have it to you by such and such a time." Liars usually have to add a promise, because they know their simple word isn't enough. Both Jesus and James addressed this issue (see Matthew 5:37 and James 5:12).

Christians should never have to promise to do anything. If they say they will do it, they will do it. Their word is their bond. Psalm 15 should be inscribed on the walls of character for every man and woman of God:

> LORD, who may abide in Your tabernacle? Who may dwell in Your holy hill? He who walks uprightly, and works righteousness, and speaks the truth in his heart; he who does not backbite with his tongue, nor does evil to his neighbor, nor does he take up a reproach against his friend; in whose eyes a vile person is despised, but he honors those who fear the LORD; he who swears to his own hurt and does not change; he who does not put out his money at usury, nor does he

take a bribe against the innocent. He who does these things shall never be moved.

The godly person "swears to his own hurt and does not change." That means he will keep his word, even if it hurts him to do so. We can't afford not to keep our word, because if we let an unsaved person down by not doing what we said, it greatly damages our testimony. We must be blameless in the eyes of the world.

Perhaps you sometimes neglect to keep your word after telling your children that you would do something. I hope you will change that—for your testimony's sake and for the sake of your children. If you don't keep your word (that is, you are a liar), more than likely neither will your children keep their word. Teach them Psalm 15. Always keep your word, and instruct them to do the same.

Only What's Yours

The Tenth Commandment is, "You shall not covet" (Exodus 20:17). This means we shouldn't desire things that belong to others.

Back up the eighteen-wheeler candy truck and grab a load (or some baby carrots). Ask one of your children to count out ten pieces on a plate and give them to you. Smile with heartfelt gratitude as he does so and thank him sincerely. Be very sweet. Next, have him count out eleven pieces and give them to your spouse. Stare at her plate. Become serious as you count your candy out loud, then count hers. Look angry, and say, "She has more than I do!" Snarl, tip over your plate, and stomp out of the room.

After a moment come back in and ask them, "What was wrong with what I did?" Explain how the sin of covetousness opens the door to all sorts of other sins—anger, jealously, hatred, and even murder. Turn to the story of King Ahab in 1 Kings 21:1–16, and read or summarize it. This story illustrates the stupidity and childishness of coveting. Ask your children if they have even been guilty of this sin.

Explain that coveting shows an ingratitude toward God for what He has given us. Not satisfied with what we have, we think we deserve something more—so we covet something before we steal it; we covet someone before committing adultery, etc. Turn with your kids to the incident in 2 Samuel chapter 11 where David coveted another man's wife before committing adultery with her. As you read about David's sin with Bathsheba, offer your kids a piece of candy for each time they spot where David broke one of the Ten Commandments. I will help you out here so that you can look good in front of your children.

> As David looked at Bathsheba, he *lusted* after her (seventh). He *coveted* her (tenth). He *slept with* her (seventh). He *stole* another man's wife (eighth). He was then *deceitful* (ninth). He *murdered* Uriah (sixth). He *dishonored* his parents' name by his terrible sin

124

(fifth). He failed to keep the *Sabbath* holy (fourth)—
how could he keep it holy when he had done such evil
things? His sin gave occasion for the enemies of the
Lord to *blaspheme* (third). His actions showed that he
didn't put God first in his life (first). He obviously had
an *idolatrous* understanding of God, revealed by his
brazen sin (second).

Ask your kids if they have ever been guilty of wanting
something that belongs to others.

The Whole Thing

The Bible says that the Commandments can be summed up
as loving God with all of your heart, soul, mind, and strength,
and loving your neighbor as yourself (Mark 12:29–31). I'm
sure you are familiar with a story Jesus told—the parable
that is normally called the "Good Samaritan." A man picked
up a beaten stranger, tended to his wounds, and carried him
to an inn. He then provided money for his care and told the
innkeeper that he would cover all the man's expenses.

That's a picture of how God *commands* us to treat our
fellow human beings. We are to love them as much as we
love ourselves—whether they are friend or foe. In fact, Jesus
didn't call the helper in that story the "good" Samaritan. He
wasn't good; he was merely carrying out the basic requirements of the Law. Love does no harm to a neighbor and is
the fulfillment of the Law (Romans 13:10). Ask your chil-

dren, "Have you always loved everyone as much as you love yourself?"

Who of us can say that we have met this requirement and are therefore free from sin? The Scriptures say *all* of us have sinned: "There is none righteous, no, not one; there is none who understands; there is none who seeks after God" (Romans 3:10,11).

Now gather a large mirror, a hammer, and some lipstick. Draw a small square on the mirror. Then tell your children, "I'm going to break this mirror with the hammer, only inside the small square!" Pull back the hammer, then ask, "Should I?" Hopefully, the kids will say, "Don't do it!" They should be able to see that you can't break one part without breaking the whole thing.

Turn to James 2:10 and read, "Whoever shall keep the whole Law, and yet stumble in one point, he is guilty of all." (There's another good memory verse.) Tell your children that God's Law is like a mirror. When we break one part of it, we break it all.

Explain that the Bible says the Law of the Lord is perfect (see Psalm 19:7). If your kids have broken even one Law, that's like dropping a perfect vase and cracking it—they have shattered its perfection.

The Stopped Mouth

Y OU HAVE NOW informed your children of God's holy standards and revealed His true character. Jesus instructs us to "be perfect, just as your Father in heaven is perfect" (Matthew 5:48). In holding up the mirror of the Law, you have shown them how they have failed to meet the standards God demands. The Bible says, "Who may ascend into the hill of the LORD? . . . He who has clean hands and a pure heart" (Psalm 24:3,4). Only those who are pure in heart will see God (see Matthew 5:8).

Your children's response at this point will reveal their hearts, so question them. Are they perfect, pure, holy, just, and good? Where do they think they will spend eternity? Scripture tells us, "Now we know that whatever the law says, it says to those who are under the law, that every mouth may be stopped, and all the world may become guilty before God. Therefore by the deeds of the law no flesh will be justified in His sight, for by the law is the knowledge of sin" (Romans 3:19,20). Once the Law has been used to show a person his sin, he will no longer attempt to justify himself before God; he now knows that he stands guilty before God and is without excuse.

Do your children have "stopped mouths"? Can you see signs of contrition (sorrow for sin)? Is there obvious guilt? Is there fear that they have angered God? Do you detect humility of heart? If so, give them the good news of the gospel. You have given them salt, so they are thirsting for righteousness; now give them living water. You have shown them that they have the disease of sin; now give them the cure of the cross.

Hopefully, you share your faith regularly and are able to do this. You should know how to present the work of the cross—that God sent His Son to suffer and die in our place. Use the example of civil law and explain that we broke God's Law, and Jesus paid our fine. Personalize it for your children by telling a story about a friend of theirs who got into serious trouble with the law, but his father willingly sold his house to raise the money to pay his fine. Explain that this is similar to what God did for them, and that Jesus rose from the dead and defeated death so they could be saved from hell.

The following illustration may help you explain the concept of someone taking their punishment in their place:

> An African chief heard about a mutiny being planned in his tribe. In an effort to quash the revolt,

he called the tribe together and said that *anyone* caught in rebellion would be given one hundred lashes *without mercy*. A short time later, to the chief's dismay, he found that his own brother was behind the revolt so he could be head of the tribe.

Everyone thought the chief would break his word. But being a just man, he had his brother tied to a tree. Then he had himself tied next to him, *and he took those one hundred lashes across his own bare flesh, in his brother's place.* In doing so, he not only kept his word (justice was done), but he also demonstrated his great love and forgiveness toward his brother.

To Pray or Not to Pray

What should you do if you think one of your children is repentant? Should you lead him in what's commonly called a "sinner's prayer" or simply instruct him to seek after God? Perhaps the answer comes by looking to the natural realm.

As long as there are no complications when a child is born, all the doctor needs to do is *guide the head.* The same applies spiritually. When someone is "born of God," all we need to do is guide the head—make sure that the person *understands* what he is doing. In the Parable of the Sower, the true convert (the "good soil" hearer) is the one who hears "and understands." This understanding comes by the Law in the hand of the Spirit (see Romans 7:7; John 16:8). If a child is ready for the Savior, it is because he has been drawn by God (see John 6:44). He will then understand that his sin grieves God and will desire to turn from it. This is why we must be careful to allow the Holy Spirit to do His work, and not rush in where angels fear to tread. Praying a "sinner's prayer" with someone who isn't genuinely repentant may leave you with a spiritual stillborn on your hands.

A Convicted Criminal

For that reason, it's essential, as you go through the Commandments, that you not be openly sympathetic with your children, or with anyone else you witness to. Sometimes it's tempting to say, "I used to lie too," to console the person. But if you do so, you may remove that most necessary of ingredients: conviction. The person to whom you are speaking is a convict, a criminal—a Lawbreaker who has so offended God that He has called for the death penalty. The individual must be made to realize that he is personally responsible for his sins.

It's the world's way to pass the blame on to someone or something else. I read recently where scientists were blaming obesity on evolution. That's nonsense. Obesity is the result of overeating, which comes from lack of self-control. If we overeat, it's because our appetite is bigger than our belly. But that won't last long. The belly expands if we stretch it.

So be sure you don't console your children in their sins. Imagine if my son stole a watch, and I asked him, "Son, did you steal that watch?" Then I quickly admitted, "I stole watches when I was a child too...all the time." That would remove from him the personal responsibility and sense of guilt for his crime. I would be sending the message, "Don't be too concerned about this, son—*everybody* does it."

When Nathan stood before David, he didn't say, "David, you took your neighbor's wife as your own. I've done that too." No. Nathan was there as a representative of God. He had been commissioned by the Lord to bring a sober message of warning to the king, and his own experience was irrelevant. He knew that every man must give an account of himself to God, and if David didn't take personal responsibility for his sin and find a place of true repentance, he would end up in hell. Have the same resolute attitude when you speak about sin with your children.

Therefore, rather than *lead* your child in a prayer of repentance, it is wise to encourage him to pray himself. When Nathan confronted David about his sin, he didn't lead the king in a prayer of repentance. If a man committed adultery and his wife is willing to take him back, should you have to write out an apology for him to read to her? No. Sorrow for his betrayal of her trust should spill from his lips. She doesn't want eloquent words, but simply sorrow of heart.

The same applies to a prayer of repentance. The words aren't as important as the presence of "godly sorrow," which the Bible says "produces repentance leading to salvation"

(2 Corinthians 7:10). The child should be told to repent—to confess his sins and turn from them. He could do this as a whispered prayer, then you could pray for him. If he's not sure what to say, perhaps you could help him use David's prayer of repentance as a model (see Psalm 51), but his own words are more desirable.

The Necessity of Repentance

Again, salvation involves turning *from* sin *to* the Savior. As Paul stated, we must exercise "repentance toward God and faith toward our Lord Jesus Christ" (Acts 20:21). Numerous Scriptures make it clear that repentance is not an optional part of salvation. The first word publicly preached by both John the Baptist and Jesus was, "Repent" (Matthew 3:2; 4:17). Jesus also said, "Unless you repent you will all likewise perish" (Luke 13:3), and God Himself "commands all men everywhere to repent" (Acts 17:30).

However, it is fashionable in Christianity today to tell sinners that "repentance" is merely "a change of mind." The word used in the New Testament for repent is *metanoéō*, which means to change one's mind, resulting in a change of action.

The Bible says,

> Seek the LORD while He may be found, call upon Him while He is near. Let the wicked forsake his way, and the unrighteous man his thoughts; let him return

to the LORD, and He will have mercy on him; and to our God, for He will abundantly pardon. (Isaiah 55:6,7)

Isaiah saw fit to tell sinners to forsake their "way" and their "thoughts." This change of mind and actions is seen in Proverbs 28:13: "He who covers his sins will not prosper, but whoever *confesses and forsakes* them will have mercy" (emphasis added). Mark 1:14,15 from the Amplified Bible shows what Jesus meant when He told sinners to repent:

Now after John was arrested and put in prison, Jesus came into Galilee, preaching the good news (the Gospel) of the kingdom of God, and saying, The [appointed period of] time is fulfilled (completed), and the kingdom of God is at hand; repent (have a change of mind which issues in regret for past sins and in change of conduct for the better) and believe (trust in, rely on, and adhere to) the good news (the Gospel).

In Acts 14:15 Paul didn't tell idolaters to simply change their mind about their sins. He told them to *turn from* their sins *to* God:

"Men, why are you doing these things? We also are men with the same nature as you, and preach to you that you should *turn from these vain things to the living God*, who made the heaven, the earth, the sea, and all things that are in them ..." (emphasis added)

A Christian is someone who has repented and trusted Jesus Christ as Lord and Savior. Those who are deceived into thinking that they can have Jesus as Savior without having Him as Lord (and there are many) will find themselves calling Him "Lord, Lord," on the Day of Judgment. He will then say to them, "I do not know you...Depart from Me, all you workers of iniquity [those who didn't turn from sin]" (Luke 13:27).

God forbid this should happen to your beloved children. Don't hesitate to use the Law to show that sin is exceedingly sinful, so that your children will tremble before a just and holy God. Spurgeon, the Prince of Preachers, speaks of the attitude one should have when coming to the Savior:

> No sinner looks to the Savior with a dry eye or a hard heart. Aim, therefore, at heart breaking, at bringing home condemnation to the conscience and weaning the mind from sin. Be not content till the whole mind is deeply and vitally changed in reference to sin.

Since no one can come to Christ unless the Father draws him, if a holy God is drawing your children to Christ, He will also draw them to holiness and away from their sin. If there is no change in reference to sin, there can be no genuine salvation. In the next chapter we will look closer at what will motivate the lost to turn from their sin.

Chapter Ten

The Monster Slayer

EARLIER, WE identified the "monster" of evil that exists in each of our darling children (and us). To slay this monster within their hearts, the Bible has given us a powerful weapon, which Jesus tells us how to use.

In Luke 12:1–5, after a confrontation with the Pharisees, Jesus calls His disciples close to Himself and says:

> "Beware of the leaven of the Pharisees, which is hypocrisy. For there is nothing covered that will not be revealed, nor hidden that will not be known. Therefore whatever you have spoken in the dark will be heard in the light, and what you have spoken in the ear in inner rooms will be proclaimed on the housetops. And I say to you, My friends, do not be afraid of those who kill the body, and after that have no more that they can do. But I will show you whom you should fear: Fear Him who, after He has killed, has power to cast into hell; yes, I say to you, fear Him!"

I wonder if, like me, you have read that passage and given it a thoughtless "Amen." Jesus said it, therefore "Amen" to it. But think about what you have just read. (I trust that familiarity didn't cause you to skip reading the verses.) He first told His disciples to beware of the "leaven" of the Pharisees, which He identified as hypocrisy. Leaven (yeast) puffs up, and that's exactly what hypocrisy does.

Ask anyone who professes to know God, but whose life doesn't match his claims, if he thinks he is a good person. No doubt he will tell you that he is morally upright. I have had many people say, "I'm a very good person." One man even told me, "I'm the best." I was impressed that I had found the most moral man on earth. However, when probed with the Law, each person (including him) proved to be a liar, a thief, and an adulterer at heart. They were puffed up with a sense of their own goodness, until the Law did its work in humbling them by showing their true state before God.

Jesus then explained that God is the ultimate witness to every crime. He is also the judge and the executioner. Every idle word that men speak they will give an account of on the Day of Judgment (see Matthew 12:36). Nobody will be getting away with anything. Not one murder—not even a lustful thought—will go unpunished.

The Meat Knife

Next, Jesus said that we shouldn't fear him who can kill the body. Think about that for a moment. How could someone kill your body? Perhaps a ruthless murderer could attack you with a fifteen-inch stainless steel serrated meat knife, plunging it into your chest with such force that it comes out in the middle of your back. Imagine seeing the unspeakably horrific sight of warm blood surging from your chest in your final seconds of life. Thoughts of such a man attacking you are horrendous! But Jesus said not to fear him. Amen?

Or this man could wrap his strong, calloused fingers around your tender throat and take two long minutes to cut off your air supply, strangling you to death. Imagine the feeling of panic that would grip you. Blood vessels burst in the eyes of those who die by such a means. *But Jesus said not to fear him.*

Don't fear him? These scenarios don't make me *fearful,* they *terrify* me, and that terror comes from my God-given instinct to survive. But Jesus said not to fear him who can kill the body. What did He mean?

Swallow the Gnat

The Master Teacher often used hyperbole in His teachings. In contrasting love with hate, gnats with camels, hot with cold, He used extremes to emphasize a point. Exaggerations can paint powerful pictures on the walls of dull human minds. This, in essence, is what He was saying:

> Does the thought of having a sharp knife thrust through your chest scare you? Would a vicious mur-

derer strangling the life out of you terrify you? That fear is nothing compared to the unspeakable horror of facing the wrath of Almighty God on Judgment Day.

He said that it would be better to drown with a millstone tied around your neck than to face God's punishment (Matthew 18:6). The Bible warns that it is a fearful thing to fall into the hands of the living God (Hebrews 10:31). Words are inadequate to describe the terror of that Day, as Almighty God will rip guilty sinners from their graves and give them the justice they deserve.

Why then doesn't the world fear God? Because the lost have been encouraged in their cultivation of idols. The seed of idolatry is already waiting to germinate in the imagination, and modern preachers often provide a generous supply of manmade fertilizer to cause it to grow. Sadly, they feed a benevolent image of God's character with the message that Jesus will provide peace, joy, love, fulfillment, and lasting happiness. To many, the gospel has become a heavenly offer to give us a happier life than the one we have without God.

Contemporary preachers frequently teach principles of daily living. They tell you how to find victory over life's many problems, how to advance in society, how to make your marriage work, how to get along with others, how to raise your kids—they talk about anything but sin, righteousness, and judgment.

If the world has an erroneous image of God—one of a jovial Father figure—then they will live their lives accordingly, transgressing the Commandments with no thought of the consequences. In today's society it is not uncommon to hear of kids who kill their parents. Hundreds of thousands more take their own lives through suicide,[25] or kill themselves slowly with drugs and alcohol. Youth today frequently lie, hate, steal, rape, and even murder without any hesitation.

> If there is no fear of God, then there is no fear of the consequences of sin—there is no fear of Judgment Day or of eternal damnation in hell.

The reason that humanity has such a propensity to do evil is that "there is no fear of God before their eyes" (Romans 3:18). If there is no fear of God, then there is no fear of the consequences of sin—there is no fear of Judgment Day or of eternal damnation in hell. Without a fear of God, there is no restraint against evil.

The Landmine

The Bible not only identifies this monster of evil that exists in the hearts of your children and in all of fallen humanity, it then hands us the weapon that will destroy it. God's Word tells us, "By *the fear of the Lord* one departs from evil"

(Proverbs 16:6, emphasis added). This, then, is what will slay the monster of evil within us—the fear of the Lord.

If you were walking along a path and saw a landmine in front of you, you would govern your steps according to what was "before your eyes." If we have the fear of God *before our eyes*, we will govern our steps accordingly. We will stay away from all sin.

People transgress God's Law simply because they lack the fear of God. And "there is no fear of God before their eyes" because it hasn't been brought before their eyes. By removing God's Law from its message, modern Christianity has minimized the exceedingly offensive nature of sin. Sin has merely become something that *separates*, rather than what it is—a super magnetized anvil for the steel justice of a holy God. They have removed the very elements that produce the fear of the Lord.

Rarely do we hear pulpits thunder the Ten Commandments and the threat of God's future punishment. Seldom do we hear the words of Jesus: "But I will show you whom you should fear: Fear Him who, after He has killed, has power to cast into hell; yes, I say to you, fear Him!" (Luke 12:5), or the words of the psalmist: "My flesh trembles for fear of You, and I am afraid of Your judgments" (Psalm 119:120). Nor do we hear the words of Paul: "Knowing, therefore, the terror of the Lord, we persuade men" (2 Corinthians 5:11).

Therefore, make sure you cultivate a healthy fear of the Lord in the hearts of your children. Read Acts 5:1–10 to your kids and let them see how God killed a couple for lying. The incident produced fear in the hearts of those who heard of it. Pray that the same thing happens to you and your children.

Again, be sure to teach your children the Ten Commandments. Consider how the Book of Proverbs admonishes children to listen to their parents' teachings about God's Law:

> My son, keep your father's [God-given] commandment and forsake not the law of [God] your mother [taught you]. Bind them continually upon your heart and tie them about your neck. When you go, they [the words of your parents' God] shall lead you; when you sleep, they shall keep you; and when you waken, they shall talk with you. For the commandment is a lamp, and the whole teaching [of the law] is light, and reproofs of discipline are the way of life. (Proverbs 6:20–23, Amplified)

If you skip around the Law, your kids may just skip around the cross. Law before grace is God's order (see John 1:17). All those who were given grace in the New Testament already had a knowledge of sin; they had been already humbled by the Law. In teaching the Law you will simply prepare your children's heart to understand grace and mercy.

You will help them appreciate the nature of sin, and as they recognize the presence of sin in their own hearts, it will drive them to the foot of the cross.

Spurgeon said of sinners, "They will never accept grace, until they tremble before a just and holy Law." Many Christians have incorporated the Law into the gospel presentation and seen it do its wonderful convicting work. The following is typical of the letters we have received:

> Two weeks ago I used the Ten Commandments for the first time in sharing the gospel with my youth group. It was the most amazing thing I've ever seen... Kids were weeping and coming to the altar to repent ... I've never seen that kind of brokenness.

If you want your children to govern their steps according to a proper fear of the Lord, have them memorize the Ten Commandments. Our children's book, *The Way of the Master for Kids*, will help you do this.[26]

This Fear Leads to Life

Most of us have favorite Bible verses. One of mine is Proverbs 19:23. Read it two or three times and meditate on this incredible promise from God:

> The fear of the LORD leads to life, and he who has it will abide in satisfaction; he will not be visited with evil.

Do you want your children to live? Do you want them to be saved from death and hell? Then teach them the fear of the Lord. It will lead them to the Savior, to the One who is the way, the truth, and the life. Without the fear of the Lord, the Ten Cannons of God's Law are unloaded. I have no fear of unloaded cannons; they can't do me any harm. Preaching the Ten Commandments and telling your children that *God is going to judge the world by that righteous standard* should put the fear of God into them so they will "depart from evil." It should cause the Law to act as a schoolmaster to bring them to Christ, and once they abide in Him, they will be satisfied. They will not "want," because the Lord is their shepherd.

Look at the last part of this promise: "He will not be visited with evil." God will work all things out for good (see Romans 8:28). He will do for your children what He did for Joseph: what was meant for evil, God turned out for his good. What more could you want for your children? So if you love them, teach them the fear of the Lord. You will never regret it.

Worldly Guests

D O YOU REMEMBER what it was like to fly before smoking was banned on airplanes? It was horrible. Breathing recycled air was bad enough without having to endure second-hand smoke. Of course, the airlines provided a smoking "section": smokers were confined to the back five rows. Unfortunately, the smoke was not. This concept was about as effective as putting a 747 beside a pulpit during a church service and revving the engines, while a sign advises that the noise should be confined to the front five pews.

Don't ever be deceived into thinking that you can allow the pollution of the world to enter your home and not contaminate your family. You won't be able to confine it. Someone emailed me an article by Jeremy Archer in which he spoke of having allowed some worldly guests to enter his home. While their behavior was questionable, they entertained his family, and he justified the friendship by saying that Jesus was accused of being a friend of sinners. Sometimes the conversations revolved around drinking, violence, drugs, the occult, sex, theft, lying, and other vices. But he said that they justified it because it was all discussed in an entertaining manner.

Their guests were having a growing influence on his family. As time passed, the behavior grew worse. Then people began partying, making obscene gestures, and even started having sex right in front of him and his family. As I read the article I remember thinking, *How could he let this happen... in front of his family! How could he be looking at them!* Then I read the final words of the article. He concluded, "Together we turned off the television."[27]

So many professing Christians allow their families to be polluted in the name of entertainment. Some Christians, realizing how their children are being affected, get rid of the TV altogether. Others learn the art of self-control, and then control the remote control. Whatever you do, *be in control.* If you have the liberty to watch television, make sure you watch only that which is governed by Philippians 4:8:

> ...whatever things are true, whatever things are noble, whatever things are just, whatever things are pure, whatever things are lovely, whatever things are of good report, if there is any virtue and if there is anything praiseworthy—meditate on these things.

Even then, you may leave your kids watching a wholesome program, but the inserted advertisements may be filthy.

So be extra careful that the world doesn't corrupt them through this means. When the mud flows, shut the door.

The world says that you can't shelter your children from wickedness. While that may be true, you can certainly give it a good try. What sort of parents would let their children roam around outside knowing that vicious dogs were loose in the area? It's your responsibility to protect them. That doesn't mean your children become monks in a monastery. It simply means that, as their parents, you keep them away from those things that you know will harm them. God sees innocence as a virtue, not a vice, so keep your children innocent toward that which is evil (Romans 16:19).

Even those things that seem good may have harmful effects. For example, it was because of my own moral convictions that I had to turn down a friend's request for a commendation on a video he had produced. It was a powerful exposé on the subject of rock music. He not only revealed the evil behind the music, but he used the Ten Commandments as a schoolmaster to bring sinners to the Savior. It was wonderful.

The problem was, when he got to the Seventh Commandment, he showed how sexually explicit rock musicians were. I wrote him a letter saying:

> We have the most tender of folks using our material. Recently a father wrote to us and said that his 13-

year-old son confessed to him that he was tempted in the area of lust, *when he watched one of our videos.* It was a two-second scene of a woman wearing shorts and a bikini top. His father said that it may seem trivial to us, but he was thrilled (and rightly so) that his Christian son had such a tender conscience. He asked that we remove the piece, and in light of Paul's not eating meat if it caused his brother to stumble, we removed it.

I realize that you have a dilemma in wanting to show how sexually explicit rock music has become, but even at my age I had to look away a number of times, because my heart is so wicked.

I'm sorry I can't put my name to it. The production itself is excellent.

God instructs us to set nothing wicked before our eyes (Psalm 101:3), and to not do anything that would cause anyone—especially a child—to stumble. Are you careful to monitor the types of entertainment that come into your home?

That includes keeping a very close watch on the music you allow your children to have—even professed Christian music. Much of it simply comes from the world's musicians who have seen big bucks in gospel music. They have tossed a few clichés and the name of Jesus into their music, and naïve Christians buy into it and let their children feed on it.

Most kids spend several hours a day being influenced by television and music. One way to keep your children from spending much time indulging in questionable entertainment is to give them responsibilities around the home. This will also prepare them for the real world that they will have to face. My daughter and her husband use family devotions to teach their children responsibilities such as how to make guests welcome in the home, how to answer the phone politely, how to always keep a godly attitude—to honor the Lord in all of life's circumstances.

Also be aware of the types of friends your children have. If they are from non-Christian families, make sure your kids are influencing them with the gospel, rather than them influencing your children with the things of the world. Peer pressure can greatly sway kids when it comes to musical tastes, fashions, attitudes toward drugs, sex, etc. This is why you need a good, communicative relationship with them. Ask your children what their friends talk about and what they believe. Pray with them for their friends' salvation.

Filling Their Minds

As much as we try to protect our kids from harmful pollutants within the home, we often overlook one tremendous source of influence outside our walls—where our children spend the majority of their waking hours.

In June 2004, a Southern Baptist General Convention resolution proposed that Christian parents pull their children out of secular schools. Many Christian parents believe they should place their children where they can be a positive influence on their non-Christian classmates. But in reality, does it usually work out that way? Supporters of the resolution said, "Many Christian children in government schools are converted to an anti-Christian worldview rather than evangelizing their school mates." A news story on the issue stated, "Additionally, the resolution cites a 2002 report by the Southern Baptist Council on Family Life that claims, '88 percent of children raised in evangelical homes leave church at the age of 18 never to return.' They blame this backsliding on government schools."[28]

In the early 1980s our children went to a secular school. One day Jacob informed me that the school was teaching lessons on the subject of the occult. I complained to the principal, who didn't seem too upset about my concerns. So, much to his shock and dismay, Sue and I took our kids out of public school and sent them to a Christian school.

We didn't have the money to cover the entrance fees and uniforms when we made the decision, but it was miraculously provided within a day of our making the commitment. Nowadays, even many Christian schools aren't what they should be, so you may need to seriously consider home schooling.

If you are sending your children to a secular school, do you realize that you are handing them over to the world? You are saying to the ungodly, "Train up my child." Consider the goal of the humanistic, atheistic, relativistic, evolutionary agenda promoted by the secular world in which we live:

> I think that the most important factor moving us toward a secular society has been the educational factor. Our schools may not teach Johnny how to read properly, but the fact that Johnny is in school until he is sixteen tends toward the elimination of religious superstition. The average American child now acquires a high school education, and this militates against Adam and Eve and all other myths of alleged history. —P. Blanchard, "Three Cheers for Our Secular State," *The Humanist*

> Education is thus a most powerful ally of humanism. What can a theistic Sunday school's meeting for an hour once a week and teaching only a fraction of the children, do to stem the tide of the five-day program of humanistic teaching? —*Humanism: A New Religion*, 1930

> Fundamental parents have no right to indoctrinate their children in their beliefs. We are preparing their children for the year 2000 and life in a global one-world society, and those children will not fit in. —Senator Paul Hoagland, 1984

> Give me your four-year-olds, and in a generation I will build a socialist state. —Vladimir Lenin

On our "The Way of the Master" television program, in an episode on how to witness to someone who is homosexual, a group of homosexuals can be seen marching together, arms linked in unity, chanting, "We're here; we're gay; we're in the PTA!"

The great theologian Martin Luther, over four hundred years ago, issued these wise words of warning:

> I advise no one to place his child where the Scriptures do not reign paramount. Every institution in which men are not increasingly occupied with the Word of God must become corrupt...I am much afraid that schools will prove to be the great gates of hell unless they diligently labor in explaining the Holy Scriptures, engraving them in the hearts of youth.

God, who seeks godly offspring (Malachi 2:15), instructs parents to teach their children to love Him with all of their heart, soul, strength, and *mind* (Luke 10:27). Is the information your children receive in a secular school filling their minds with truth and teaching them a biblical worldview —or an anti-biblical one?

In Deuteronomy 6:6–9 God further commands parents:

> And these words which I command you today shall be in your heart; you shall teach them diligently to your children, and shall talk of them when you sit in your house, when you walk by the way, when you

lie down, and when you rise up. You shall bind them as a sign on your hand, and they shall be as frontlets between your eyes. You shall write them on the doorposts of your house and on your gates.

In his book *Excused Absence*, Douglas Wilson asks regarding this command:

> What do those children hear when they *sit* down at desks purchased by the taxpayer? That men are evolved from primordial goo, that *Heather Has Two Mommies*, and that all we need to do is to make sure we recycle. What do they hear when they *rise up*? Assorted blasphemies and foul language on the playground. What do they read when they *walk by the way*? A big sign at the entrance of the school proclaiming that it is a drug-free zone.
>
> In short, the very thing God requires in Deuteronomy 6 is patently ignored by parents who send their children to government schools. For much of their waking hours, the only words these children hear are the words of men who live in opposition to the Word of God.[29]

Remember, it is the Christian parents' responsibility to bring up their children in the training and admonition of the Lord (Ephesians 6:4). Be sure you protect your children from all ungodly influences—both inside your home and out.

Fools, Because of Their
Transgressions are Afflicted

Previously, I mentioned the concept of offering your children incentives. Michael Reagan said that his father had offered him and his siblings the incentive of $500 if they wouldn't smoke cigarettes or drink alcohol until age twenty-one. He said he made it until he was eighteen. He offered his own daughter the same incentive (plus inflation), and ended up writing a check for $5,000 when she turned twenty-one.

You may not have the resources to be able to offer that sort of incentive to your kids. Besides, I think there is a better way. We can follow the example of Scripture. The Book of Proverbs is very liberal in its use of the words "fool," "foolish," and "stupid" in describing humanity. And Psalm 107:17 points out, "Fools, because of their transgression, and because of their iniquities, were afflicted." We need to impress upon our children that any restrictions God places on our behavior are there for our good. Help them see that avoiding drugs and alcohol and abstaining from premarital sex are based not just on biblical guidelines but on good common sense.

Instead of just telling our kids to stay away from alcohol, we should show them how stupid it is to drink. Any chemist will tell you that alcohol is a poison (it's toxic). When someone is in-*toxic*-ated, he is "poisoned." The body protests with confused thinking, slurred speech, and impaired vision, memory, and judgment. The victim vomits. The next day his head throbs with pain, yet he still drinks the poison.

Hundreds of thousands of innocent people have been maimed on the roads by drunk drivers, and untold numbers have been killed, yet the world cannot bring itself to say, "Don't drink." It can only say, "Don't drink and drive." Perhaps this is because (as it has been well said) alcohol is the only enemy that man has succeeded in loving. It destroys his liver, heart, and kidneys. It gives him high blood pressure and causes blood vessels to burst in his skin. It entices him to beat his wife and abuse his kids. It will eventually destroy his ability to enjoy the intimacies of the marriage bed. It is a killer, yet he still drinks.

Alcohol isn't a stimulant as many suppose, but is a suppressant that reduces the drinker's inhibitions. It dulls the naggings of his conscience so that he can commit sexual and other sins that he wouldn't indulge in while sober. It leads him to lie to those he loves. A man who gives himself to the demon of alcohol becomes a slave to its addictive properties; he bows his knee to its dictates. Hard liquid is called a "spirit." How applicable. As he throws back a "shot" he may as well be doing it with a gun. Alcohol mocks him —it steals his dignity and takes control of his will. The Bible says, "Whoever is led astray by it [and there are millions] is not wise" (Proverbs 20:1).

Then there are those brainless folks who think they are cool when they burn dried plants and suck the smoke into their lungs. Imagine an animal climbing onto a roof and placing its mouth over the top of a smoking chimney so it could breathe in the smoke. What creature in the whole of creation would be so stupid as to do that? Only man. He has his own little smoking chimney that he wraps his silly lips around and inhales the smoke. But unlike that of a wood fire, this smoke contains carcinogens—deadly poisons. Here are some of the effects these poisons have on the human body:

> Tobacco is often associated with heart disease and lung cancer, but its deadly carcinogens are also risk factors for a number of other life-threatening illnesses … "If you smoke, it's estimated, you have ten times the risk of getting head and neck cancer than if you didn't smoke. That's true for lung cancer, too," says Erich Sturgis, M.D. "Combining heavy alcohol use with smoking increases the risk even more." Head and neck cancer includes cancers of the tongue and mouth, nasal cavities, voicebox, throat, and esophagus (tube leading from the throat to the stomach).[30]

The fumes also contain nicotine—an addictive drug that takes over the human will. Smokers don't consider the consequences of their dirty habit. They would be better off to daily poke their eye with a sharp needle, more and more each day, until the eye fell out of its socket. That would have far less fearful consequences than what they are doing with their lungs. They somehow imagine that they are breathing the polluted air into a couple of bags that simply take in the smoke and then let it out.

You want to rid your kids of that ignorant notion. Go to the library and find a book describing how intricately God has made the lungs, and what they do for the body.[31] Look at magnified photos of the lungs, showing how their tiny holes take in air, filter it, and send it through the blood to the brain.

Perhaps you could get a new sponge and compare it to a really old, grimy sponge, explaining that when we put smoke into our lungs we are clogging up the tiny breathing holes, polluting them, and making our lungs look like the dirty old sponge. Tell your children that smoking causes a disease called "emphysema." Have them remember the word, and say it to themselves when they see someone smoking.

Explain that the world often calls drinking and smoking "vices." Get hold of a vise and have each of your children place a finger in it, while you tighten it slightly. Tell them that that's what happens with a "vice." The two may be spelled differently, but they do the same thing.

Bring Death to Life

Perhaps the following example will bring this concept to life. Have your kids keep their mouths closed tightly, and with their forefingers press hard against the outside of one nostril and softly against the other, just letting in a tiny amount of air with each breath. The sound of each breath should be clearly heard coming through the nostril.

Then have them hold their breath for twenty or thirty seconds (as long as possible), while still holding their fingers tightly against one nostril and lightly against the other. When they start breathing again, they are to breathe only through the one nostril that is letting in the tiny amount of air. *Remind them not to open their mouths or let air through the other nostril.* Let them feel the panic of not being able to breathe, just for a second or two. Then explain that that's what smoking will lead to. Emphysema will cause that same panic, twenty-four hours a day, seven days a week, until it suffocates them to death—the only cure for this horrific disease. It would be far less painful to lose an eye than to die through suffocation. It is like an endless drowning.

Then turn to John 10:10 and read Jesus' warning that we have an enemy who came to steal, kill, and destroy. How true that is, just through this one means. Millions die each year as a direct result of breathing poisonous cigarette smoke into their precious lungs. They do this despite the fact that it will give them a terrible taste in their mouths, brown teeth, bad breath, and prematurely aged facial skin; and despite the clear warning label on the package that it is harmful to their health.

You may also want to gather cigarette advertisements from popular magazines and point out how smokers are portrayed using images of tough, manly cowboys, or of clean-cut, healthy young people enjoying surfing or skiing. Ask your kids why cigarette companies would use such images, and why they spend so much on advertising. What's their motive?

Fritz Gahagan, once a marketing consultant for five tobacco companies, offers this insight into his business:

> The problem is how do you sell death? How do you sell a poison that kills 350,000 people per year, 1,000 people a day? You do it with the great open spaces ...the mountains, the open places, the lakes coming up to the shore. They do it with healthy young people. They do it with athletes. How could a whiff of a cigarette be of any harm in a situation like that? It couldn't be—there's too much fresh air, too much health—too much absolute exuding of youth and vitality—that's the way they do it. [32]

If it wasn't so tragic, it would be laughable. Cigarette smokers are dumber than the dumbest of dumb sheep.

Then there are those folk who have sex outside of marriage. They not only sin against God, against their conscience, and against their own body (1 Corinthians 6:18), but they also open themselves up to sexually transmitted diseases (STDs), including the horror of AIDS.

Prior to 1960 there were only two sexually transmitted diseases that were prevalent; today there are around two dozen. At least *one in four* people will contract an STD during their lifetime, with two-thirds of all STDs occurring in people under age twenty-five.[33]

The U.S. has the highest rates of STDs in the industrialized world, with an estimated 15.3 million new cases reported each year. And those are just the cases that are reported—less than half of the population has ever been tested for any form of sexually transmitted disease. STDs often don't show symptoms, yet they can still be transmitted to others even when no symptoms are visible.

Several STDs are incurable; some are fatal. STDs can result in irreparable lifetime damage, including infertility, pelvic inflammatory disease, potentially fatal ectopic pregnancies, chronic pelvic pain, cervical cancer, paralysis, heart disease, brain damage, and death. They can also cause blindness, bone deformities, mental retardation, and death for infants infected by their mothers during gestation or birth.

Outside of marriage, there is no such thing as truly "safe sex"; the only way to completely eliminate all risk of contracting a sexually transmitted disease is abstinence—to save sexual activity for one lifetime partner within the bounds of marriage, as God intended.

Explain to your children that sexually transmitted diseases are a direct result of going against God's Law, and that these diseases are merely the temporal consequences in this life. For fornicators and adulterers, there are far more terrible eternal consequences in the next.

Sin's Pleasures

It's important to teach your kids that the Christian life is one of self-denial. The Bible doesn't hide the fact that sin is exciting (see John 3:19; 2 Timothy 3:4), and the need to deny the pleasure of lust in particular will become evident as the child grows sexually aware. Yet we must learn to deny ourselves certain pleasures because we know that they are not pleasing in God's sight.

There is a story about a small boy who was sent to bed, then five minutes later he called out, "Da-ad..." His father called back, "What do you want?" He said, "I'm thirsty. Can you bring me a drink of water?" The father responded, "No. You had your chance earlier. Lights out."

A few minutes later the boy said, "Da-aaaad..." "What?" "I'm really thirsty. Can I have a drink of water??" His father replied, "I told you no! If you ask again, I'll have to spank you!"

Several minutes passed. "Daaa-aaaad..." "What!" "When you come in to spank me, can you bring me a drink of water?"

Sometimes the thirst for sin is all-consuming, and there are some who imagine that the sweet satisfying waters of sin's pleasures will outweigh the spanking of hell. That is the ultimate lie. Such thinking comes from a mixture of a little unbelief, some idolatry, and a lot of stupidity. The fading memory of the delights of an adulterous fling find little room in the mind of a person with a severe toothache, a serious burn, or even a badly stubbed toe.

I have never physically committed adultery but I have been burned when I touched a hot toaster, had a raw nerve poked by a dentist's drill, and have seriously stubbed a toe, and I can testify that the pain leaves no room for any thought but the pain. So, be sure you teach your children Bible verses that teach them the reality of hell. Let them know that hell isn't going to be a nice place, and that no amount of sinful pleasure in this life will ever be worth the torment of hell for eternity.

Your Greatest
Weakness

A S I MENTIONED EARLIER, your own personal example of how to live the Christian life will perhaps have the greatest influence on the spirituality of your children. If you are evangelistically minded, that will impress upon them what a biblical Christian should be like. Demonstrate a deep concern for all those who are on their way to hell, and pass that concern on to your children by speaking often of the terrible fate of the ungodly. Soberly pray with your children for the unsaved and then follow through by verbally sharing your faith, making it a habit to pass out gospel tracts. We have tracts that are so delightful, so unique, that non-Christians ask for more. If you have never given out tracts, please consider this easy means of getting the gospel into the hands of the lost.[34]

If you are not evangelistically inclined, let me ask you a question. What would you think of a man who sees a neighbor's child fall into his swimming pool, but who has no concern? He's busy waxing his car and if he is interrupted by having to save some kid, the shine will spoil.

As he polishes his car and watches the terrified child drown, he is not only morally guilty, but is also guilty of a serious crime—what is defined in civil law as "depraved indifference." Those words are very descriptive: a *depraved* state is about as low as you can go, and *indifference* means that you couldn't care less.

If you don't care about the salvation of those around you, if you have no concern for the lost, you are guilty of depraved indifference. Love could never be so cold-hearted as to polish a car while a child drowns. The thought is repulsive. And a Christian cannot profess to know the love of God in Christ, and yet be unconcerned about the horrible fate of those who die in their sins. The very thought is repulsive. If you are apathetic about the lost, or reluctant to witness due to fear, put this book down, go somewhere quiet, and ask God to forgive you. Then plead with Him to give you a love that will swallow your fears, and a gratitude for the cross that will forever banish the sin of indifference.

Have you noticed that when you turn on a light, darkness leaves? The two are incompatible. It's the same with fear and love. Love casts out fear (see 1 John 4:18). When we turn on the light of God's love, fear must leave. The key is to let love cause you to think of the terrifying fate of the person to whom you want to witness.

Paralyzing fear isn't from God, but it can work for your evangelistic good by making you rely on Him. Fear shows us that we are weak, causing us to call on God for His help. So instead of allowing your fears to discourage you, let them drive you to Him who gives courage, and in so doing, your greatest weakness then becomes your greatest strength. Conquering your own fears about witnessing will help you to influence your children in the way they should go.

What's the Score?

Sue and I enjoy the fast-moving, tough, heart-stopping sport of rugby, so we were excited when our oldest son, Jacob, gave us a videotape of a game he had recorded. We planned to view the tape that afternoon after a trip to the mall.

As I walked into an interesting men's clothing store at the mall, I handed a foreign-looking gentleman a Million Dollar Bill tract, telling him that he was doing a good job. He loved it. He also loved another tract that looked like a business card, but said "Department of Annoyance—Director." He followed Sue and I around the store, laughing and joking with us, asking Sue how she put up with me.

When he discovered we were originally from New Zealand, the subject of rugby came up, and he immediately blurted out, "New Zealand's team is wonderful. Man, did they beat England yesterday!" Then he gave us the score! It was amazing—we had been living in the U.S. for fifteen years and hardly a soul had mentioned the game. Here we were, about to enjoy a game within the hour, and a stranger told us the outcome.

Actually, it didn't bother me. If I didn't know the score, I would have gotten a little tense if it was a close game. Once I knew our team won, I wouldn't get as stressed out, no matter how well the opposing team played.

That's why I don't get too upset when I get persecuted, laughed at, or rejected for my faith. When the game gets tough, I'm not worried because I know how it ends. God wins out over the world and the devil, and it is an unspeakable consolation to know that I am on the winning side. Many, however, will *not* be on the winning side when the game is over. Have you thought about their fate?

Sue told me that she had cried as she watched the televised funeral of President Reagan. The most moving part was when Mrs. Reagan rested her head on the casket of her beloved husband. He was gone, snatched from her arms. One could only imagine her grief at losing a loved one.

Yet the same scenario is played out *millions* of times each year. Every minute of every day, there are grief-stricken multitudes who whisper an unspeakably painful goodbye to those they love. An incredible 150,000 people die each and every 24 hours.

I cannot imagine the anguish of losing a loved one outside of Christ. They are truly gone *forever*. Do you ever think about losing your loved ones? It's a frightening thought, but a reality we all must face. What are you doing so that your separation isn't forever?

Never forget that you have an enemy who would like you to ease off a little on your concern for the lost, or to leave the Ten Commandments, Judgment Day, the cross, repentance, and faith out of the presentation. He's the one whom the Bible calls the "accuser of the brethren." Be ready for his discouraging whispers. The enemy doesn't want you to share your faith with your children, let alone with strangers. He came to "steal, kill, and destroy" your children. Think about that. Are you going to let him do that? All it takes is for you to ignore the spiritual realm when it comes to your kids. Ignore that which is unseen and live for the seen. Just go with the flow—feed on modern movies, despite their blasphemy, violence, and sex. Indulge in sexually explicit, godless music and gossip magazines. Simply follow the sinful ways of this world, and take your children with you. It is an easy path to hell.

Are you creating children of God who will know salvation from death, or children of the devil who will know the terrors of hell? Do your children love righteousness, or are they enjoying the pleasures of sin? Have you cultivated the fear of the Lord, or have you fed them an insipid image of a god who isn't to be feared? Have you overemphasized God's love and omitted His wrath? Then you may reap the terrible consequences of idolatry. Do your children use His name lightly and read His Word flippantly, or do they tremble for fear of Him? Are you leading them into a lifestyle of being true and faithful witnesses? Do they know the terror of the Lord and thus persuade men? Are you genuine in your walk with God or are you a self-serving hypocrite, a Judas—deceived and deceiving?

I can think of no greater tragedy than to lead my children into a professed faith in Christ that lasts only until Judgment Day. Imagine having your beloved children cry, "Lord, Lord!" and hearing Jesus say to them, "I do not know you...Depart from Me, all you workers of iniquity" (Luke 13:27). Never take parenting lightly. Each of us has the most sobering of responsibilities.

Let me close with this email from a mother who couldn't understand why her children "fell away" from the Lord, before she discovered the key to winning souls:

> In March 2004, I was really mourning as I saw my two oldest children walking away from the Lord... What is wrong? We had devotions every day as a family, and we home schooled them in Bible, God, and character every day. Then I found your book *Revival's Golden Key*,[35] which I've read twice. Now I embrace the true gospel! God had used His Law in my life to save me; however, I lost it somewhere sitting in church pews for 30 years! Now I embrace *all of God*—His Law

and His grace! Heaven and hell! His judgment and His mercy! Now I have *all* of the Bible! Now I know what to give my two oldest children! Now I can go to the lost with the Law and win souls!

Thank you! Thank you! Thank you! I have found what I needed. Now my soul is racing to reach the lost.

As Charles Spurgeon said, the Law is our "ablest auxiliary"—our most powerful weapon—in the gospel proclamation. Having such a weapon in our arsenal will give us the boldness and confidence we need to reach the lost. Let's be faithful to use it to bring our children (and others) to Christ...and keep them there.

Conclusion

I GREATLY APPRECIATE the fact that you have taken the time to read this book. I am sincerely honored that you would consider using some of the principles I have related in the raising of your kids. But if there is one thing that I hope you will take to heart, it's the importance of you as an individual Christian having a love for the lost. Seeking first the kingdom of God and His righteousness will carry in its wake your children's best interest.

If you fear God enough to obey Him and have concern for the salvation of your neighbors, how much more will you have a burden for the salvation of your children? They will be primary in your concerns when it comes to eternal issues. You will therefore diligently establish a family altar, pray together, keep them from harmful influences, etc. And as you do so you can trust God to work in the lives of your children to draw them toward the Savior. And be assured, if your children truly come to the safety of the Savior in genuine repentance, God will keep them there. He is able to keep them from falling and present them faultless before the presence of His glory, with exceeding joy.

> *Now to Him who is able to keep you from*
> *stumbling, and to present you faultless before*
> *the presence of His glory with exceeding joy, to God*
> *our Savior, who alone is wise, be glory and majesty,*
> *dominion and power, both now and forever.*
> *Amen.*
> JUDE 24,25

Notes

1. For a thorough explanation of this teaching, see *The Way of the Master* by Kirk Cameron and Ray Comfort (Tyndale House Publishers).
2. See *Out of the Comfort Zone* by Ray Comfort (Bridge-Logos Publishers) for the full story.
3. Dr. Robert A. Morey, *How to Keep Your Faith While in College* (Southbridge, MA: Crowne Publications, 1989).
4. Stuart Scott, "One Thing I Have Desired," *Praise 7*, Maranatha! Music, 1984, 1986.
5. Charles H. Spurgeon, *Come, My Children: A Book for Parents and Teachers on the Christian Training of Children* <www.biblebb.com/files/spurgeon/cyc02.htm>.
6. We have included a number of anecdotes in *The Evidence Bible* (Bridge-Logos Publishers).
7. Jeffrey Dahmer <www.tornadohills.com/dahmer/quotes.htm>.
8. Spurgeon, *Come, My Children* <www.biblebb.com/files/spurgeon/cyc09.htm>.
9. These are available at www.livingwaters.com.
10. See *The Evidence Bible* (Bridge-Logos Publishers).
11. Charles H. Spurgeon, *Spurgeon's Sermons Volume 54: 1908*, "God's Providence" (Grand Rapids, MI: Christian Classics Ethereal Library) <www.ccel.org/ccel/spurgeon/sermons54.all.html>.

12. To learn more about how to use the Law in evangelism, go to our website (www.livingwaters.com) and listen to free instructional messages.

13. The "Foundation Course" is the first eight episodes of the television program "The Way of the Master" with Kirk Cameron and Ray Comfort, which teaches Christians how to share their faith biblically. It is available through www.livingwaters.com.

14. For a more thorough teaching on true and false conversion, you may like to read *The Way of the Master* by Kirk Cameron and Ray Comfort (Tyndale House Publishers).

15. This very important message can be heard at www.livingwaters.com/listen.shtml.

16. Now titled *The Way of the Master* by Kirk Cameron and Ray Comfort (Tyndale House Publishers).

17. See *What Did Jesus Do? A Call to Return to the Biblical Gospel* by Ray Comfort (Genesis Publishing Group).

18. C. H. Spurgeon, "The Perpetuity of the Law of God," *Metropolitan Tabernacle Pulpit*, #1660, p. 285.

19. J. C. Ryle, *Holiness* (Cambridge: James Clark, 1952).

20. Spurgeon, *Come, My Children*.

21. Peg Tyre, Julie Scelfo, and Barbara Kantrowitz, "The Power of No," *Newsweek*, September 13, 2004, p. 42.

22. Those with a Roman Catholic background may not be familiar with this Commandment, as the traditional Catholic catechism removed it, and the Tenth Commandment was split into two to make up the difference.

23. Spurgeon, *Come, My Children*.

24. Josephson Institute of Ethics, "Report Card on the Ethics of American Youth," 2004 <www.josephsoninstitute.org/Survey2004/>.

25. See www.1000deaths.com.

26. For other tips on helping kids memorize the Ten Commandments, see the episode "How to Witness to a Family Member" in the series "The Way of the Master" (which contains an animated

teaching), as well as a free resource "Teach Kids the Ten Commandments" on our website (www.livingwaters.com).

27. Jeremy Archer, "The Unruly Houseguests," *Discipleship Journal*, January/February 2004, Iss. 139.

28. Kyle Williams, "Baptists Missing the Mark," *WorldNetDaily*, June 12, 2004 <www.worldnetdaily.com/news/article.asp?ARTICLE_ID=38924>.

29. Douglas Wilson, *Excused Absence: Should Christian Kids Leave Public Schools?* (Mission Viejo, CA: CruxPress, 2001), p. 59.

30. "Tobacco Use Can Cause More Than Lung Cancer," *CancerWise*, November 2003 <www.cancerwise.org/november_2003>.

31. Or see "How Your Lungs Work" by Craig C. Freudenrich, Ph.D. <www.howstuffworks.com/lung.htm>.

32. Quoted in *World in Action*, Secrets of Safer Cigarettes, 1988.

33. Information in this section is taken from the CDC National Prevention Information Network <www.cdcnpin.org/scripts/std/std.asp>, and the University of Pennsylvania School of Medicine <www.med.upenn.edu/ucclinic/apreducation.html>.

34. See www.livingwaters.com.

35. Now titled *The Way of the Master* by Kirk Cameron and Ray Comfort (Tyndale House Publishers).